Teaching With Favorite
Leo Lionni Books

BY KATHLEEN M. HOLLENBECK

SCHOLASTIC
PROFESSIONAL BOOKS

JAN 4 2003

NEW YORK • TORONTO • LONDON • AUCKLAND • SYDNEY
MEXICO CITY • NEW DELHI • HONG KONG

For Alan, who illuminates my life.

▲ ▲ ▲ ▲ ▲ ▲ ▲ ▲ ▲ ▲

*Special thanks to the author, Leo Lionni,
for the grace and depth of his work,
and to Deborah Schecter,
whose enthusiasm and expertise helped shape this book.*

Acknowledgments & Credits

"Snail's Pace" from *ALWAYS WONDERING* by Aileen Fisher (A Charlotte Zolotow Book). Copyright © 1991 by Aileen Fisher. Used by permission of Marian Reiner for the author.

"Fish" by Mary Ann Hoberman from *YELLOW BUTTER PURPLE JELLY RED JAM BLACK BREAD* by Mary Ann Hoberman. Copyright © 1981 by Mary Ann Hoberman. Reprinted by permission of Harcourt Brace and Company.

"Yellow" by David McCord from *AWAY AND AGO: RHYMES OF THE NEVER WAS AND ALWAYS IS* by David McCord. Copyright © 1968, 1974 by David McCord. Reprinted by permission of Little, Brown and Company.

The following are used by permission of Knopf Books for Young Readers, a division of Random House:

Photograph of Leo Lionni (page 5). Book jacket and interior illustrations (top of pages 21–25) from *Swimmy* by Leo Lionni. Copyright © 1963 by Leo Lionni. Book jacket and interior illustrations (cover, page 4, and top of pages 27–30), and mouse illustration (pages 19, 25, 30, 36, 43, 48, and 55) from *Frederick* by Leo Lionni. Copyright © 1967 by Leo Lionni. Book jacket and interior illustrations (top of pages 32–36) from *The Biggest House in the World* by Leo Lionni. Copyright © 1968 by Leo Lionni. Book jacket and interior illustrations (cover, page 12, and top of pages 39–43) from *Fish Is Fish* by Leo Lionni. Copyright © 1970 by Leo Lionni. Book jacket and interior illustrations (cover and top of pages 45–48), butterfly illustration (pages 2, 3, 6, 17, 22, 28, 33, 40, 46, and 52), and background for "This Book's Message or Theme" (pages 16, 21, 27, 32, 39, 45, and 5l) from *It's Mine!* by Leo Lionni. Copyright © 1986 by Leo Lionni. Book jacket and interior illustrations (top of pages 51–55) from *Nicolas, Where Have You Been?* by Leo Lionni. Copyright © 1987 by Leo Lionni. Book jacket (page 58) from *Six Crows* by Leo Lionni. Copyright © 1988 by Leo Lionni. Book jacket (page 59) and interior illustrations (top of pages 16–19) from *Alexander and the Wind-Up Mouse* by Leo Lionni. Copyright © 1969 by Leo Lionni. Book jacket (page 60), interior illustrations (top of pages 51–55), and background for "Let's Talk About It," "Head Off on a Word Hunt!" and "Share a Poem" (pages 17–19, 22–23, 25, 28–30, 33, 35, 36, 40–41, 43, 46–48, 52–53, and 55) from *A Flea Story* by Leo Lionni. Copyright © 1977 by Leo Lionni. Book jacket (page 62), interior illustrations (top of pages 2–13 and 58–64), and caterpillar illustration (pages 18, 23, 29, 35, 41, 47, and 53) from *The Alphabet Tree* by Leo Lionni. Copyright © 1968 by Leo Lionni. Book jacket (page 63) from *Tico and the Golden Wings* by Leo Lionni. Copyright © 1964 by Leo Lionni.

The following are used by permission of Astor-Honor Publishers:

Book jacket (page 16) from *Little Blue and Little Yellow* by Leo Lionni. Copyright © 1959 by Leo Lionni. Book jacket (page 61) from *Inch by Inch* by Leo Lionni. Copyright © 1960 by Leo Lionni.

Front cover and interior design by Kathy Massaro
Interior illustrations by Maxie Chambliss with additional artwork by James Graham Hale

ISBN: 0-439-04388-3
Copyright © 1999 by Kathleen M. Hollenbeck
All rights reserved.
Printed in the U.S.A.

Contents

About This Book 4

About Leo Lionni 5

Exploring the Books of Leo Lionni: Teaching Activities for Any Time 6

Little Blue and Little Yellow: A Story for Pippo and Other Children 16

Swimmy 21

Frederick 27

The Biggest House in the World 32

Fish Is Fish 39

It's Mine! 45

Nicolas, Where Have You Been? 51

Ideas for Use With Other Leo Lionni Books 58

    Six Crows 58

    Alexander and the Wind-Up Mouse 59

    A Flea Story 60

    Inch by Inch 61

    The Alphabet Tree 62

    Tico and the Golden Wings 63

Additional Resources 64

About This Book

With prose and pictures, author-illustrator Leo Lionni speaks to the heart, mind, and conscience of the child. Woven in a rich tapestry of color and design, his stories amuse, educate, and inspire. As plots unfold, so does Lionni's exploration of techniques in painting, sculpture, paper cutting, printwork, and more. He intertwines visual art with the timeless arts of music, poetry, and drama, reflecting his own passions and igniting desire in others. More than a simple picture book, each of Lionni's tales is a work of art with a message and a mission for young readers.

The activities in this book are designed to bring out the message and the mission while strengthening skills in all subject areas, heightening awareness of techniques in illustration and design, and challenging children to take what they can and apply it to their lives. With these activities, children will learn helpful techniques for problem-solving, conflict resolution, and handling emotions. They'll explore animal life and behavior, and experiment with techniques in collage, printmaking, painting, sketching, patterning, and construction. They'll use imagination and creativity and hone skills in written and oral expression. Above all, children will study and strengthen such qualities as integrity, kindness, self-control, generosity, compassion, and compromise—values that cannot be reinforced early or often enough.

Beginning on page 6, you'll find activities designed to be used with any and all Leo Lionni fables. These activities provide ideas for analyzing story elements, creative writing, graphing, art, and critical thinking, as well as a reproducible game. Seven of Leo Lionni's most popular picture books are featured in the main portion of this resource. These are *Little Blue and Little Yellow*, *Swimmy*, *Frederick*, *The Biggest House in the World*, *Fish Is Fish*, *It's Mine!*, and *Nicolas, Where Have You Been?* A section at the back of the book (see page 58) features activities to extend other Leo Lionni stories, including *Six Crows*, *Alexander and the Wind-Up Mouse*, and *Inch by Inch*.

In its simplest form, this book is a resource of activities meant to help children experience and extend the stories of Leo Lionni. At its core, it is a guidebook to exploration of the arts and human behavior. As Leo Lionni used Frederick to bring life to winter, use this resource to bring his stories to life in your classroom.

About Leo Lionni

Author-illustrator Leo Lionni

*L*eo Lionni was born in 1910 in Watergraafsmeer, a small community just outside Amsterdam. The son of an accountant and an opera singer, he was born into a close-knit family and was drenched in a culture of art, music, and architecture from the start. Pad in hand, young Leo spent hours studying and sketching the paintings that filled the museums near his home. From his bedroom on the top floor of an apartment house, he absorbed details of a Chagall that hung in the hallway nearby. Describing the painting as "a happy canvas with cheerful colors that seemed to flutter like ribbons in an icy wind," Lionni indicates the painting may have been "the secret birthplace of all the stories I ever wrote, painted, or imagined." (From *Between Worlds: The Autobiography of Leo Lionni.* Knopf, 1997, pp. 12–13)

In fact, Leo Lionni's bedroom itself might have been the birthplace. In cages and containers across the room lived snails, caterpillars, fish, frogs, and mice that Lionni loved to tend— creatures that would one day reappear on the pages of his fables.

Early years in Amsterdam led to life in Brussels, Philadelphia, Genoa, Zurich, and Milan. In 1939 he moved back to the United States with his wife and two sons, where he first worked in advertising and then became art director of *Fortune* magazine in New York City. Lionni found great success at *Fortune* and was in constant contact with prominent artists of the day. Yet in time Lionni himself would be known as a prominent artist, leaving *Fortune* for a farmhouse in Italy and publication of his first picture book, *Little Blue and Little Yellow*, in 1959.

This first of Lionni's stories came to life on a train ride as a tale he created on the spot to entertain his young grandchildren. Tearing scraps from a magazine, Lionni brought two characters to life and told a story that would travel far beyond the moving train. Now, 40 years and many, many picture books later (including four Caldecott Honor award-winners), Leo Lionni continues to create work that entertains and expresses his need—and his knack—for seeing beauty in everyday life. As Lionni says of his favorite character, Swimmy: "Little by little, conditioned by the events of his life, he discovers the meaning of beauty as a life force and finally assumes his role as the eye who sees for the others." (From *Frederick's Fables: A Treasury of 16 Favorite Leo Lionni Stories.* Knopf, 1997, page xii)

Throughout his lifetime, Leo Lionni has seen and experienced beauty in artwork and in human nature. And in his picture books, he imparts that vision and insight to us, the fortunate recipients.

EXPLORING THE BOOKS OF LEO LIONNI:
Teaching Activities for Any Time

▲▲▲▲▲▲▲▲▲▲▲▲▲▲▲▲▲▲▲▲▲▲▲▲▲

Many of Leo Lionni's tales fall into the genre of literature known as the fable. Brief tales with a big message, fables seek to teach readers a lesson in values and behavior, using animals as instructors by example. Fables, unlike proverbs, deliver their messages in story form. While some are as brief as half a page, the fables of Leo Lionni extend to picture-book length, providing a satisfying story with a strong, solid message.

The following activities can be used with any Leo Lionni fable. Some can be used on the spot, whereas others require preparation. Peruse this section to find activities that best serve your goals and available time.

Activities in Language Arts

☼ **Explore Fables by Aesop and by Arnold Lobel** Bring the fables of both Aesop and Arnold Lobel into your classroom. Invite children to compare these fables with the fables of Leo Lionni.

☼ **Write a Fable** As a class, work together to write your own fable. Decide on the message you'd like to convey, and then create characters, a plot, and a satisfying ending. Bind the story by placing its pages in a stack and stapling along the left side. Make a cover by folding gift wrap, wallpaper, fabric, or contact paper over the pages, and staple in place along the same edge. Cut colorful duct tape to the length of the book, and fold it over the edge to cover the staples.

☼ **Change the Story** How would *Little Blue and Little Yellow* have been different if either of the characters had found a red friend? Let children rewrite parts of any story to add a different twist to the tale.

☼ **Make Story Sacks** On index cards or slips of paper, draw pictures that represent characters or events from a story. Put the pictures in a lunch bag and label it with the title of the story. During free time, children can choose a bag and retell the story by putting the pictures in order. Provide extra bags for children to make their own story sacks, and encourage children to take the bags home to share with their families.

☼ **Make a Story Time Line** Provide drawing paper and crayons or markers. Have each student draw a different scene from the same Lionni story. Then hang a clothesline across one wall in the room, and use clothespins to hang children's illustrations in the order each scene took place in the story. You might also want to make a time line using one long strip of butcher paper. Have children work in groups to illustrate various events along the time line.

☼ **Write a Diary Entry** Ask children to pretend to be one of the characters in the story. Have them write or draw a diary entry in response to something that happened in the story.

☼ **Develop a New Character** Let children work in small groups to create, name, and develop a new character for one of the stories. Urge children to pay attention to details and  describe the character's emotions, family life, appearance, interests, and so on. Then have children rewrite a portion of the story to introduce the new character or use the character in a story of their own.

☼ **Make a Travel Poster** Provide children with drawing paper and crayons or markers and have them make a poster of a place that a character from a story might see. For example, the frog in *Fish Is Fish* might see a billboard for a dairy farm where he could go to see cows.

☼ **Write a News Bulletin** Let children pretend they were on hand to see the frog save the fish's life in *Fish Is Fish* or to watch as the birds brought berries to Nicolas and his friends in *Nicolas, Where Have You Been?* Ask children to describe the incident in writing as a news story or on cassette as a news broadcast. Younger children might want to describe the incident by drawing it.

☼ **Write a Riddle** What has fins but wants to walk? The fish in *Fish Is Fish!* Challenge children to write riddles of their own about different story characters.

☼ **Make Comic Strips** Using characters and events from the stories of Leo Lionni, let children draw and write their own comic strips to tell existing stories or to create their own sequels.

Activities in Science

☼ **Make a Terrarium** Use a small glass fishbowl to make a terrarium modeled after a scene in one of the stories. Line the bottom of the bowl with soil. Let children place twigs, leaves, rocks, shells, berries, or other natural items inside the bowl to create an environment similar to one in *Frederick; It's Mine!;* or *Nicolas, Where Have You Been?* Encourage children to draw and cut their own snails, frogs, mice, or fish out of tagboard and place them in the terrarium.

☼ **Look for Patterns in Nature** Review the story illustrations in search of repeating patterns: leaves on a twig, rocks in a cluster, flowers in a garden, petals on a flower, and so on. Then take a nature hike outside, urging children to find similar patterns in nature. For a lasting remembrance, place grasses, flowers, leaves, twigs, clover, and other bits of nature between paper towels. Then place heavy books on top and set aside for several weeks, until dry. When dry, glue to construction paper and laminate to make bookmarks, gift tags, and cards that children can give as gifts.

☼ **Classify the Animals** Make a chart to classify the animals from Leo Lionni's stories. Which animals fly? Swim? Crawl? Have two legs? Four legs? Wings? Are nocturnal? Hibernate? Make loud/quiet sounds? Eat leaves? Eat meat?

☼ **Make an Animal Shape Book** Cut paper in the shape of a character from one of Leo Lionni's stories. Staple six pieces of paper together to make a book. On each page, have children write one fact about the animal: where it lives, what it eats, whether it is nocturnal, whether it hibernates, and so on.

Activities in Art

☼ **Make a Book Jacket** Ask children to design a new book jacket for the story, using construction paper and crayons or markers. Encourage them to foreshadow the theme of the story in their illustration.

☼ **Make a Story Mask** Give children paper plates, and ask them to draw a mask of a story character. Let children cut out eye holes and glue a craft stick to the bottom of the mask. Then have children hold the masks before their faces while classmates guess which characters they are pretending to be.

☼ **Make a Story Puzzle** Have students each draw one scene from the story on an 8 1/2- by 11-inch sheet of construction paper and then cut the paper into six pieces, place the pieces in an envelope, and label with their name. Have children pass the puzzle to a classmate, who can then assemble it and guess which part of the story it represents.

☼ **Make a WANTED Poster** Give each student a piece of white drawing paper. Ask children to draw a character's picture at the top and, below it, describe what the character looks like, how he or she acts, what interests he or she has, and where he or she lives.

☼ **Make Puppets** Help children make and use puppets to act out their favorite stories. For variety, try making shadow, hand, sock, or stick puppets using materials such as paper bags, cardboard tubes, socks, paper plates, wallpaper, carpet scraps, yarn, pipe cleaners, lace, seeds, straws, feathers, fabric, buttons, thread, rickrack, sequins, dried pasta, cotton, wooden spoons, felt, clothespins, corks, glitter, beads, glue, fabric paint, and craft sticks.

☼ **Make Dioramas** Ask children to bring in a shoe box. Provide clay, paper grass, construction paper, glue, pipe cleaners, felt, feathers, cotton balls, and other craft supplies. Ask children to work independently or in pairs to recreate in a box a scene from the story.

Activities in Drama

☼ **Reenact a Scene** Divide the class into groups of three or four. Ask each group to reenact a scene from one of Lionni's stories while classmates identify the story.

☼ **Play a Character Game** Have children sit in a circle. Write the name of a story character on a piece of paper. Tape the paper to one student's back, and have him or her ask classmates questions to learn the character's identity. Questions might include "Do I like berries?" "Can I fly?" "Do I climb trees?" "Am I a mouse?" You might also give children the name and have classmates question them to find out who they are.

Activities in Social Studies

☀ **Award Characters** Hold an awards ceremony for characters. Which character was kindest? Bravest? Smartest? Have children make ribbons and reward the characters for these and other attributes.

☀ **Map a Character's Neighborhood**
Provide children with drawing paper and crayons or markers. Have each student draw a map showing where a character lives in relation to other characters in the story, bodies of water, other landmarks, and so on. Encourage children to

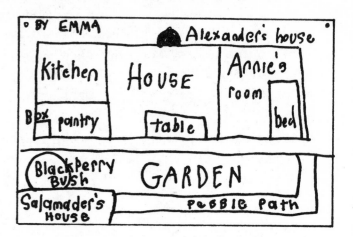

feature as many details from the story as possible, such as Alexander's hideout, the pantry, the pebble path, and the garden in *Alexander and the Wind-Up Mouse*.

☀ **Change the Setting** Emphasize the effect of one's environment on one's way of life. As a class or in small groups, students can rewrite one of the stories so that the setting is completely different. For example, the three frogs in *It's Mine* might live in a city park instead of on an island. What would they fight over: Rights to a park bench? Leftover picnic food? What would be the danger that draws them close?

Activities in Math

☀ **I See** Let students classify as they count with this guessing game. Call on a volunteer to study the illustrations in one of Leo Lionni's stories, such as *Frederick*. Ask that student to choose one illustration and describe to classmates one detail from it. Classmates must listen to the description and identify the correct illustration. For example, a student might say, "I see four groups of five different colors" to describe the scene in which Frederick's friends envision the colors he describes.

☀ **Use Shape Blocks to Tell a Story** Divide the class into pairs. Give each pair twelve pattern blocks in assorted shapes. Let partners take turns or work together, using the blocks as characters and props in a story they create as they go along.

Graphing and Charting Activities

*L*eo Lionni's fables offer dozens of graphing opportunities, relating directly to one story or comparing several. Some questions you might ask to develop a graph include:

☀ Which part of the story did you like best?

☀ Which job would you rather do if you were a mouse (gather seeds, collect berries)?

☀ What is your favorite color? Kind of weather? Time of day? Season?

Besides basic bar graphs, there are other novel ways to do graphing with children.

Picture Graph

Let children vote for their "favorites" by drawing pictures. For example, invite children to draw on an unlined index card a scene from their favorite Leo Lionni story. Let children tape their card on the graph to indicate their preference. For a simpler graph, draw a smiling face on the graph as each child names his or her favorite book.

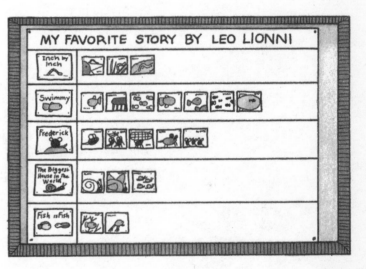

Stacked Graph

As a follow-up to *Little Blue and Little Yellow*, you might make this graph. Write "What Is Your Favorite Color?" on a piece of paper and place it flat on a table. Write the name of each category, such as "Pink," "Red," "Blue," "Purple," and "Orange," on an index card. Lay the index cards flat on the table in a row. Provide building blocks. Let each child take one block, affix a name label (using self-sticking notes), and stack it behind the index card that shows his or her favorite color.

Clothespin Graph

Cut two different-colored pieces of posterboard in half lengthwise. Tape one half of each color together. Number the left side and the right side from 1 to 15 (or higher, depending on the number of children in your class). Write children's names on clothespins. Have each child clip a clothespin to one side of the graph.

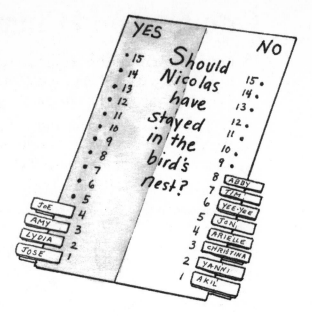

Venn Diagrams

Use a Venn diagram to compare and contrast two characters, their needs, and their actions. Draw the diagram on chart paper or a chalkboard and let children write the specifics inside. The sample diagram below compares and contrasts the fish and the frog in *Fish Is Fish*.

Frog

Breathes through lungs.

Lives on both land and water.

Has legs.

Eats bugs.

Jumps.

Swims in water.

Lives in water when very small.

Fish

Breathes only through gills.

Lives only in water.

Has fins.

Eats small fish.

Charts

☼ **Chart Animals by Size** Help children make a chart listing the animals found in various Leo Lionni books: mice, snails, fish, crows, and so on. Then ask children to list the animals in order by height.

☼ **Explore a Character's Feelings** Make a chart to explore each character's emotions throughout the story. Ask the questions: What happened? How did the character feel? How did you as the reader feel?

What Happened?	How Did Nicolas Feel?	How Did You Feel?
The bird grabbed Nicolas.	afraid	afraid, curious
The mother bird said Nicolas could stay.	relieved, happy	happy
The mice wanted to attack the birds.	worried, desperate	frustrated, sad

Mouse Manners Game

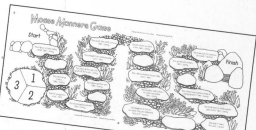

In this board game, children collect "berries" for doing good deeds.

To prepare for the game:

1. Reproduce pages 14 and 15. Line up the pages as indicated, and tape them together. Glue to lightweight cardboard for added durability.

2. Use a brass fastener and paper clip to put together the spinner as shown.

3. In a self-sealing plastic bag, place about 50 small red beads or buttons. These will serve as berries.

4. Take children outside, and ask each student to find a small rock, about one inch in diameter. Wash the rocks, place them in a resealable bag, and use them as "mouse" playing pieces. (Children might want to add mouse features with markers and attach a yarn tail.)

5. Divide the class into groups of three or four. Be sure each group has several playing pieces, 15 berries, one game board, and one number cube. (Use the pattern on page 20.)

To play the game:

1. Children take turns in alphabetical order by last name.

2. The first player places his or her mouse on START, spins the spinner, and moves the mouse the number of spaces indicated.

3. The player follows the directions written on the space.

4. The player who reaches FINISH with the most berries is the winner.

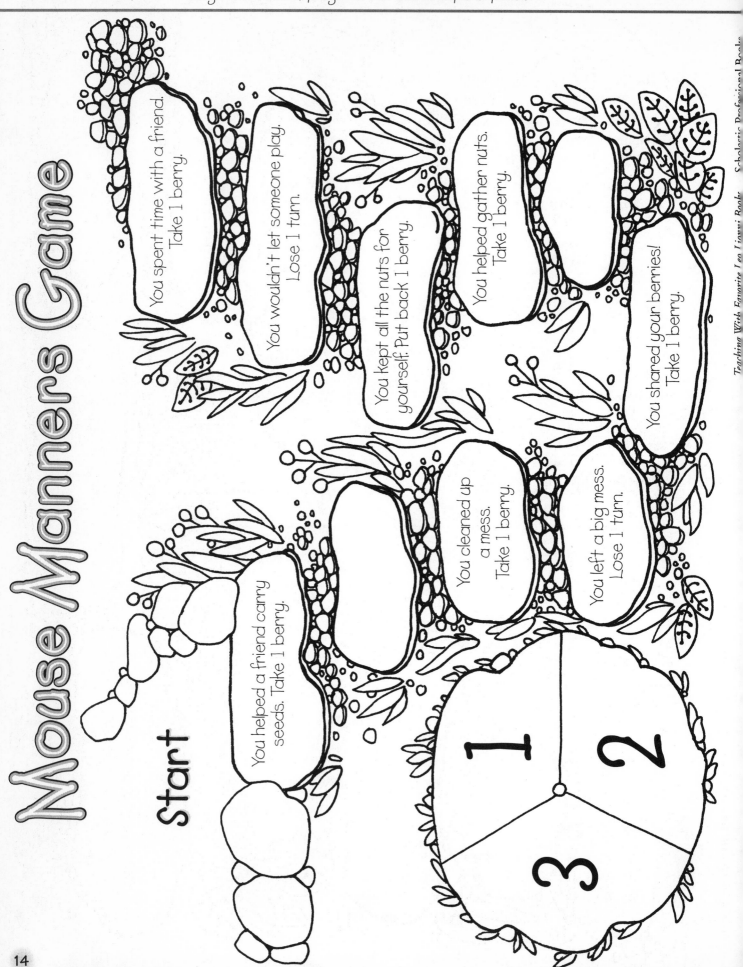

Mouse Manners Game

You spent time with a friend. Take 1 berry.

You wouldn't let someone play. Lose 1 turn.

You kept all the nuts for yourself. Put back 1 berry.

You helped gather nuts. Take 1 berry.

You shared your berries! Take 1 berry.

You cleaned up a mess. Take 1 berry.

You left a big mess. Lose 1 turn.

Start

You helped a friend carry seeds. Take 1 berry.

1
2
3

Teaching With Favorite Leo Lionni Books · Scholastic Professional Books

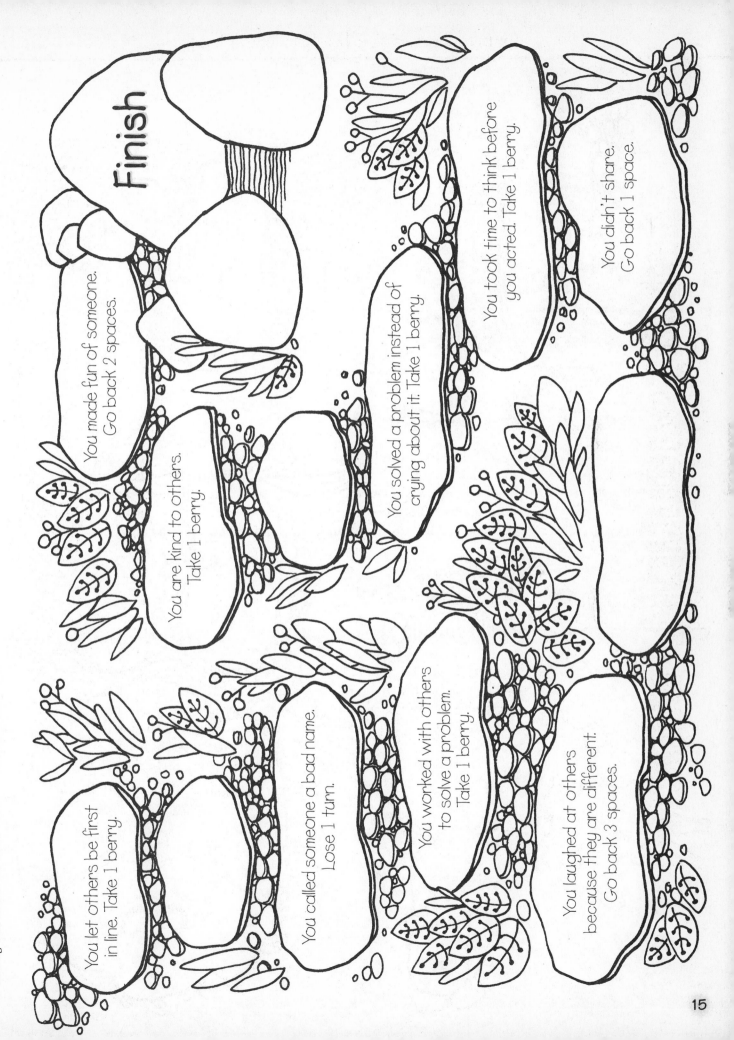

Finish

You made fun of someone. Go back 2 spaces.

You are kind to others. Take 1 berry.

You solved a problem instead of crying about it. Take 1 berry.

You took time to think before you acted. Take 1 berry.

You didn't share. Go back 1 space.

You let others be first in line. Take 1 berry.

You called someone a bad name. Lose 1 turn.

You worked with others to solve a problem. Take 1 berry.

You laughed at others because they are different. Go back 3 spaces.

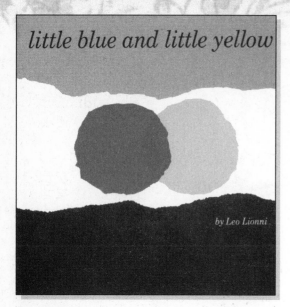

little blue and little yellow

by Leo Lionni

Little Blue and Little Yellow: A Story for Pippo and Other Children

(ASTOR-HONOR, 1959)

This Book's Message or Theme

☀ Friends come in all colors.

☀ Friends can affect each other's lives.

About the Book

In this, the first of Leo Lionni's picture books, two round blobs of color share friendship and frolic in their neighborhood. Named for their hue, Little Blue and Little Yellow embrace one day and find that their colors combine to make green. Although they do not stay green, they are forever changed by knowing that friends rub off on friends, and color proves no boundary.

Before You Read

Predicting the Story Critical Thinking

Hold up *Little Blue and Little Yellow* (as Leo Lionni refers to this book) so children can see the cover art. Then read the title aloud, and ask them to guess what the story might be about. Write their guesses on chart paper, and turn it into a graph by asking children to tell which prediction they agree with most. Make tally marks beside each prediction to show how many children chose it. After you read the story, invite children to tell which predictions were closest to the story line.

Our Guesses	Little Blue and Little Yellow: What Might This Story Be About?
a sun and a cloud	卌
different colors	卌 ‖
little things	‖‖
balloons	‖‖

Talk About the Story   Reading ◆ Language Arts

Through discussion, bring out points of interest in the story. Questions you might ask include:

- ☼ What did Little Blue and Little Yellow do for fun in their neighborhood?
- ☼ How did Little Blue and Little Yellow become green?
- ☼ What happened when Little Blue went home green instead of blue?
- ☼ How did Little Blue and Little Yellow feel when their parents didn't recognize them? Why did they feel that way?
- ☼ When did Little Blue's mama and papa find out what caused Little Blue to turn green?
- ☼ How did the families feel in the end? Why did they feel that way?

NOTE: Children may point out that Little Blue disobeyed his mama by going outside when she told him to stay home. If this comes up, take time to discuss the importance of following rules and never leaving home without a parent or guardian's permission.

Mixing Colors   Art

In the story, the artist combined blue and yellow to make green. Review and expand this color concept by letting children explore and combine colors in the following activities.

Mix Paint Divide the class into small groups. Provide each group with a paper plate on which you have placed one blob each of red, blue, and yellow paint. Let children combine colors to make different-colored circles on a separate sheet of paper. To demonstrate the process, first dip a brush in red paint and move a blob of red to an empty space on the plate. Then add to it a blob of blue paint and mix until the new blob turns purple. Other colors children might make include orange (red and yellow), green (blue and yellow), brown (green, yellow, and red), and turquoise (green and blue).

Make Paint-Blot Art Give each student one sheet of 8 1/2- by 11-inch paper. Show them how to do the following: Fold the paper in half as if making a card. Open the paper flat and drop blobs of paint on the inside fold or on either side of the fold. Fold the paper again and press gently along the outside. Open the paper to reveal the paint blot. Then ask children to write or dictate a sentence or two that gives the paint blot a name and tells a story about it.

Let's Talk About It
Critical Thinking

When Little Blue and Little Yellow became close, their colors combined to make a new color. Each friend had an effect on the other and changed him. Ask children to tell about times when someone they know has changed them in some way. For example, a parent might show the importance of being patient with others. A teacher who demonstrates kindness may prompt children to imitate kind, thoughtful acts. Be sure to advise children that not all influences are positive ones. Include in your discussion examples in which someone can actually be a harmful influence, such as a person who encourages children to litter, or to treat others roughly.

Becca

One day pink and blue bumped into each other. They became a beautiful butterfly.

Head Off on a Word Hunt!

Language Arts

Help children look through the story and find phrases that tell *where*, such as

☀ **at home**

☀ **across the street**

☀ **in school**

☀ **around a corner**

☀ **in the park**

☀ **through a tunnel**

Provide drawing paper and crayons. Ask children to draw a picture showing Little Blue and Little Yellow playing together in a location that the author did not include in the book, such as "in a sandbox," "over a fence," or "up a tree." Have children write a sentence using the location to describe their picture.

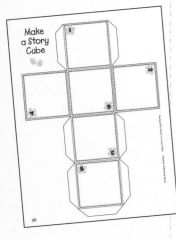

Make a Tissue Paper Collage

Help children combine shapes and colors in an intriguing collage. Ask children to cut tissue paper into shapes such as squares, circles, and triangles. Provide each student or pair of children with liquid glue or liquid starch in a small cup. Have children dip a paintbrush into the glue or starch and paint a thin layer of it on a paper plate. Let children press individual pieces of tissue paper onto the wet plate. Instruct children to paint another thin layer of glue or starch over the tissue. Have children add another layer of tissue, overlapping colors for effect. Dry completely, punch holes for hanging, and display.

Make a Map   Geography

Reread *Little Blue and Little Yellow*. Ask children to tell what Little Blue saw in his neighborhood (houses, a school, a store, a park, a tunnel, and a mountain). As a class, work together to create a map of Little Blue's neighborhood, drawing Little Blue's house across from Little Yellow's (as specified in the story) and placing other landmarks anywhere children choose to. Older children who are familiar with maps may want to work independently or in small groups. Children might also want to draw and name Little Blue's friends and/or design a home or bedroom for Little Blue. Let children practice using their maps, directing classmates to start at a specific location and "go to the playground" or "go to Little Blue's house."

Make a Story Cube   Language Arts

Photocopy page 20 for each student. Have students glue the page to lightweight cardboard, then cut out the pattern. With the story cube laid flat so the number 1 is right side up in the top left corner, have children:

1. Draw a picture in box 1 to show what happened first in the story.
2. Draw a picture in box 2 to show what happened next.
3. Flip the cube around so box 3 is right side up in the top left corner. Draw a picture in the third box.
4. Continue in this manner to complete boxes 4, 5, and 6. The sixth box should show how the story ended.
5. Fold the pattern on the dotted lines to form a cube and secure the sides with glue or tape.

NOTE: Children may find it helpful to list the six events they plan to feature before drawing them. Encourage them to do this on a separate sheet of paper. If children have never made a story cube before, you may need to walk them through the process and complete the story cube as a class. Children may also enjoy using the cubes to retell the story to classmates or bringing the cubes home to share with family members.

Make a Paint-Blot Book Language Arts ◆ Art

Invite children to create artwork in the style of Leo Lionni by making paint blots on paper and writing a story based on them. Provide children with paper, paintbrushes, and paint. Have them paint one or more blots on a page. Using the blots as characters, children can write a story.

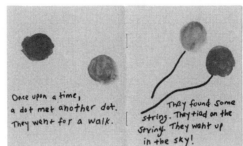

Once upon a time, a dot met another dot. They went for a walk.

They found some string. They tied on the string. They went up in the sky!

Colors at Play Critical Thinking ◆ Art

Challenge children to think of other games Little Blue and his friends might play besides Hide-and-Seek and Ring-a-Ring-O'Roses. Use paint blots or crayons to draw the activity, modeling the art after Lionni's.

Books With a Similar Message or Theme

Hamanaka, Sheila. *All the Colors of the Earth* (William Morrow & Company, 1994). Children come in all colors, and they greet life with gusto in this poetic celebration of ethnic diversity.

Henkes, Kevin. *Jessica* (Greenwillow, 1989). Ruthie and her imaginary friend Jessica are inseparable until Ruthie meets a real girl named Jessica on the first day of school.

Walsh, Ellen Stoll. *Mouse Paint* (Harcourt Brace Jovanovich, 1989). Three mice discover red, blue, and yellow paint—with colorful results!

Share a Poem
Language Arts

Yellow

Green is go,
and red is stop,
and yellow is peaches
with cream on top.

Earth is brown,
and blue is sky;
yellow looks well
on a butterfly.

Clouds are white,
black, pink, or mocha;
yellow's a dish of
tapioca.

—David McCord

Share the poem with children. Then copy it onto chart paper or a chalkboard, drawing a blank line in place of each color named. Have children read through the poem and write any colors they wish in place of the others. Ask them to draw a picture to go with the new poem.

Make a Story Cube

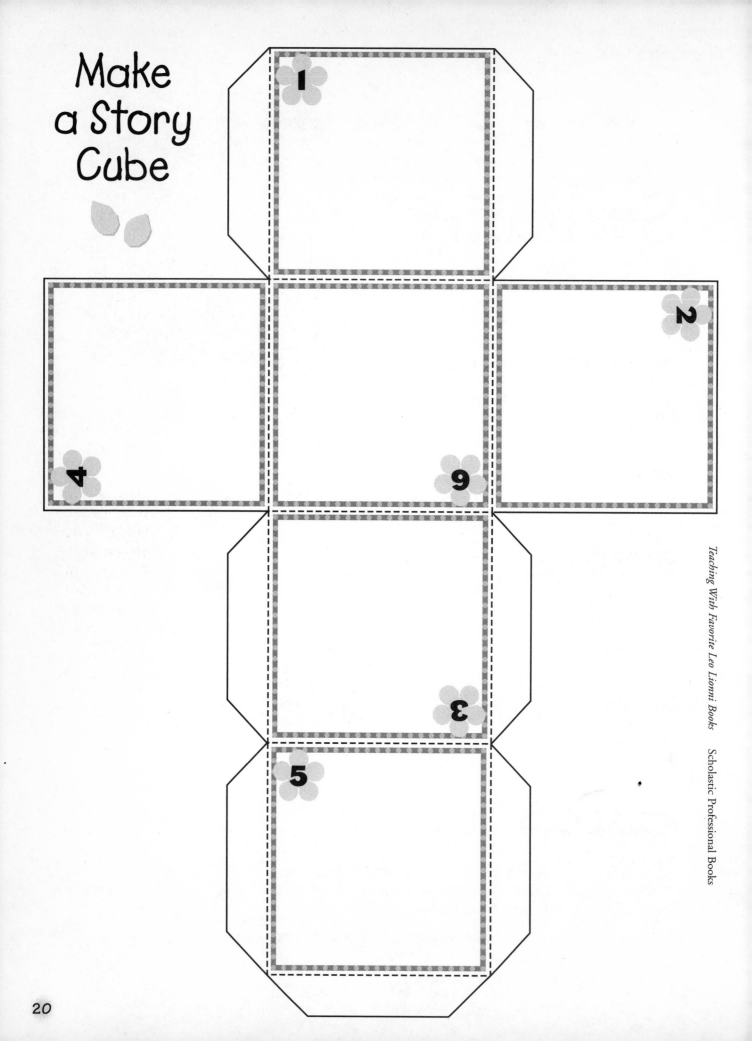

Teaching With Favorite Leo Lionni Books   Scholastic Professional Books

Swimmy

(PANTHEON, 1963)

About the Book

Separated from his family, a fish named Swimmy travels undersea alone. When he meets a school of fish who are afraid to swim in the open, he teaches them to move together in a way that wards off predators.

Before You Read

Solving Problems Critical Thinking ♦ Language Arts

Talk with children about what it means to have a problem and to solve it. Explain that problems large and small come up in daily life and that every problem has a solution, although some are easier to find than others. You may wish to give some examples of simple daily problems, such as breaking a pencil, forgetting one's lunch, or missing the school bus. Invite children to propose solutions for these. Then hold up *Swimmy* and explain that it tells the story of a fish who helped others solve a problem.

After You Read

Talk About the Story Reading ♦ Language Arts

Invite children to talk about the story. Ask:

- ☀ How did Swimmy feel when he escaped from the tuna and swam alone in the deep sea?
- ☀ What helped Swimmy feel happy again?

To get around without being eaten, Swimmy urged the fish to swim together in the shape of a big fish. Challenge children to think of another solution to the problem. Ask: "What else might the fish have done to find freedom without danger?" Let children draw different solutions on paper. Invite them to share their ideas. Accepting all ideas as worthy, invite children to vote on which one they would choose if they were Swimmy, looking for an alternative way to save the school. Ask them to give reasons for their choices.

☀ Why didn't the new school of fish want to swim and play and see things?

☀ Did Swimmy think the fish were right to lie still so they wouldn't get eaten? Why do you think Swimmy thought what he thought?

☀ What did Swimmy do to help the fish solve their problem?

☀ Why do you think Swimmy offered to be the eye of the fish?

NOTE: The author Leo Lionni has said that he identifies with Swimmy because Swimmy wanted to be the eye of the fish, the one who sees for others. In the introduction to *Frederick's Fables* (Knopf, 1985), Lionni writes, "Like Swimmy, the creator of picture books for children has the responsibility to see for the others. He has the power and hence the mission to reveal beauty and meaning."

What Would You Do? Bulletin Board Art ♦ Critical Thinking

Cover a bulletin board with blue paper for an undersea background. Then provide children with tagboard cut in the shape of a fish. (Older children may wish to cut out the fish themselves.) Let children decorate one side of the fish with paint, markers, crayon, glitter, glue, feathers, sequins, and whatever else they choose. On the other side, write or have children write a problem for others to solve. The problem might be something related to people or something related to fish. Examples of problems include:

☀ You twist your ankle in gym class.

☀ You don't like the lunch in your lunch box.

☀ You forgot to bring your library books back to school.

☀ You left your backpack on the bus.

☀ You don't know how to spell a word.

☀ A math problem seems too hard for you to do.

Use a hole punch to make a hole at the top of each fish. Then tie a 6- to 8-inch length of string through the hole. Staple the end of each string to the bulletin board so the fish hang at different heights. Staple an envelope beneath each fish. During free time, invite children to flip over a fish, read the problem, and write a solution on an index card or scrap of paper. Have them write their name on the solution and slip it in the envelope beneath the fish. At the end of the week, review the solutions and commend creative problem-solvers!

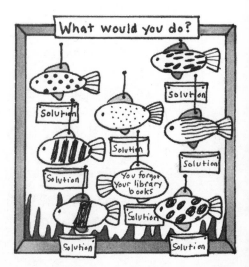

Under the Sea Art

What did Swimmy see as he traveled around by himself? Let children recreate the scene with crayons, paper, and paint. Refresh their memories by reading *Swimmy* again, emphasizing the part of the story where Swimmy is alone in the deep ocean. Urge children to close their eyes as you read this part of the story. Ask them to make a mental picture of what Swimmy might have seen underwater. Then have them use crayons to draw some of the things Swimmy saw, making sure to press hard on the crayons as they draw. When they have finished, have children paint over their drawings with blue, green, or blue-green watercolors, covering the entire page. The areas with crayon will resist paint, and the result when dry will be a translucent view of undersea life.

Make Prints Art

Review the artwork in *Swimmy*, and ask children how they think the artist might have gotten so many red fish on the page and made them all alike. Ask: "Do you think he painted each fish? Most likely, someone will guess that the artist made his own stamp to print them. Tell children that they will make stamps of their own. Encourage them to imitate Leo Lionni's technique, printing or arranging many small shapes to create one larger shape, as Swimmy and his friends did. Invite children to think of other shapes besides the one shown in the story. Ask: "What other shape might the fish have created to scare off larger fish?" Here are some suggested ways to make prints.

- ☼ Cut or buy precut sponges in the shape of letters, numbers, animals, stars, and so on. Let children dip these in paint and press on paper again and again to form a larger shape.
- ☼ Use ready-made rubber stamps. Let children press them onto ink pads and print the designs over and over.
- ☼ Let children use forks, plastic knives, or pen caps to press shapes or designs into clay or play dough. Again, repeat as needed to create a larger shape.
- ☼ Purchase or borrow hole punches that cut in a variety of shapes (snowflakes, seashells, teddy bears, and so on). Enlist the help of children, and punch a pile of shapes. Then let children use glue sticks to glue the shapes to paper to make a larger shape.

snowpile

worm

Head Off on a Word Hunt!
Language Arts

Challenge children to find words in the story that tell what Swimmy saw as he swam alone in the sea. These words include:

anemones	eel
fish	lobster
medusa	rocks
seaweed	tuna

Invite children to choose one of the words and write a story, poem, or comic strip featuring it.

Make a Story Strip   Critical Thinking

Reproduce page 26 and distribute. Help children read the directions and understand that they are to create a story strip that shows a problem they have had and what they did to solve it. Let children draw and write or dictate conversation bubbles or captions for each frame of the story. When children have finished, invite them to share their story strips. Emphasize the idea that every problem has a solution, and then have children identify which problems were easy to solve and which were more difficult.

NOTE: Extend the thinking process by asking children to generate several plausible solutions for the problem each classmate describes. For example, a student might draw himself waking up in the middle of the night. The problem: He is afraid of the dark. The solution: Turn on a light. Classmates might also suggest that the student keep a night-light on at all times or sleep with a favorite stuffed animal.

Make a Floating Jellyfish   Science ◆ Art

In the story, Swimmy saw a medusa, or jellyfish. Bring jellyfish to light for children with this simple science activity. Find a picture of a jellyfish in an encyclopedia or sea-life reference book. Let children study the picture and make observations about the jellyfish: It has tentacles that hang down, it has almost no color, it floats on the water, and so on. Then use the following supplies to help children make their own jellyfish. For each student pair or group you will need two clear plastic sandwich bags, a twist tie, scissors, tape, a clear bowl, and water. Here's what to do:

1. Cut one plastic bag into strips to make tentacles.
2. Tape the strips to the bottom of the second bag.
3. Fill the second bag about halfway with water. Then seal it with a twist tie.
4. Fill the bowl halfway with water, and lay the bag on the water so the plastic tentacles float.

Ask children to look at the "jellyfish" and make observations about it. You might ask:

- ☀ Is it easy to see the jellyfish in the water? Why do you say that?
- ☀ Why is it important for the jellyfish to be difficult to see?
- ☀ What happens to the jellyfish when we make waves in the water?
- ☀ Why do you think a jellyfish needs tentacles?

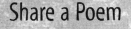

Let's Get Together Social Studies

At Swimmy's command, the little fish joined to make the shape of a big fish. Let children take turns being Swimmy and directing their classmates to stand together and form various shapes, such as a square, a circle, an arrow, a letter of the alphabet, a number, and so on. To help children get started, you might wish to outline the shape with sidewalk chalk on pavement or concrete. Then have children stand inside the lines to fill the shape. Extend the activity by having children play a game of Follow the Leader to simulate the behavior of a school of fish with a leader.

Where Did the Story Take Place? Social Studies

"A happy school of little fish lived in a corner of the sea somewhere." So begins the story of Swimmy, a little fish who soon finds himself alone in the sea. Where were those fish living? Challenge children to find probable locations, based on the sea creatures Swimmy sees in the story. Help them research where the following creatures live: tuna, jellyfish, lobster, eels, and sea anemones.

How Many? Math

Help children understand how estimation is useful for counting large quantities of items. Ahead of time, cut the top and bottom off several clean, empty half-pint milk cartons. Divide the class into several small groups. Give one carton to each group. Have children look at the illustration in *Swimmy* that shows the large school of fish. Ask them to guess how many fish there are. Then have each group place its carton on part of the illustration. The carton will serve as a frame around a portion of the picture. Have students count the number of fish enclosed by the frame. Then have them see how many times the frame will fit on the picture. Help them use that number to estimate how many fish there are in all.

Books With a Similar Message or Theme

Bradby, Marie. *More Than Anything Else* (Orchard, 1995). A young boy dreams of learning to read and in time does, with the help of his mother, a stranger, and a determination stronger than his circumstances.

Meddaugh, Susan. *Hog Eye* (Houghton Mifflin, 1995). Captured by a wolf, a young pig outwits her captor and amazes her family with tales of her escape.

Steig, William. *Dr. De Soto* (Farrar, Straus and Giroux, 1982). Dr. De Soto and his wife run a dentist's office for animals. All goes well until a crafty fox comes in with a toothache, and the De Sotos must think fast to stay out of his jaws.

Share a Poem
Language Arts

FISH
Look at them flit
Lickety-split
Wiggling
Swiggling
Swerving
Curving
Hurrying
Scurrying
Chasing
Racing
Whizzing
Whisking
Flying
Frisking
Tearing around
With a leap and a bound
But none of them making the tiniest
            tiniest
        tiniest
    sound.

—Mary Ann Hoberman

Let children find the action words in the poem. Write each word on a separate sheet of paper and hand out. Duplicate words as needed so that each child has one. Ask children to draw a picture that shows animals or objects other than fish moving in the way their word describes (worms wiggling, cars swerving, and so on).

Make a Story Strip

Draw your own story in the boxes below. Tell about a problem and what you did to solve it.

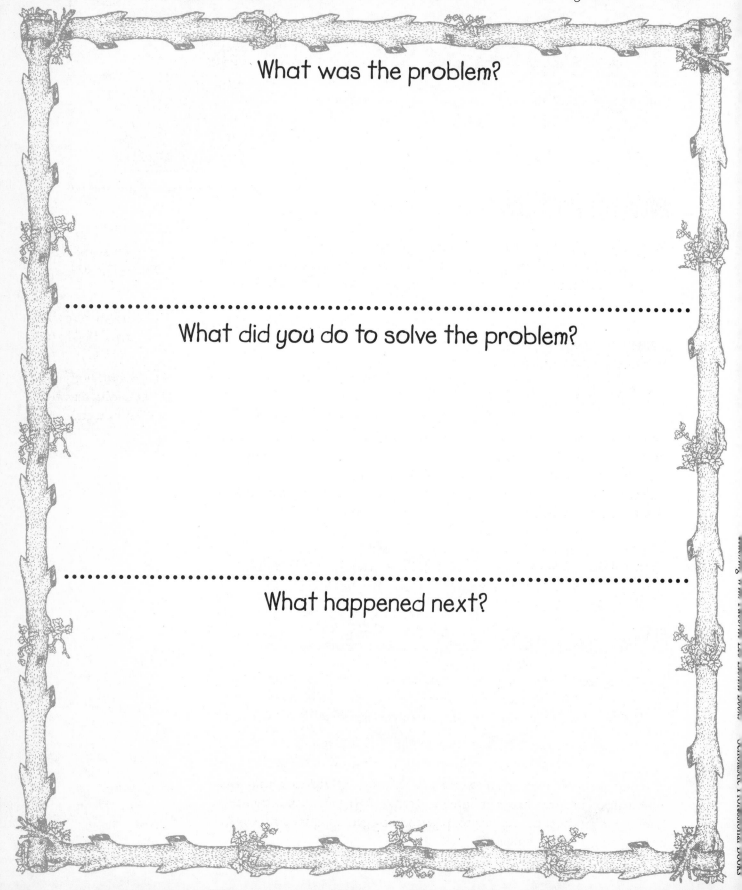

What was the problem?

What did you do to solve the problem?

What happened next?

Frederick

(PANTHEON, 1967)

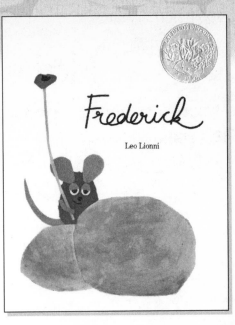

Frederick

Leo Lionni

About the Book

Frederick tells the story of a field mouse who shares dreams and memories to help cheer his friends during long winter months. Frederick paints pictures with words, demonstrating the power of language and the importance of each individual's contribution to the group.

Before You Read

Go, Groups! Social Studies

Talk about various groups to which children in your class belong: families, sports teams, scouting organizations, and so on. Ask children to choose one group and tell how they help out (doing chores, cleaning up, kicking the ball during a game) and how this helps the group. You may wish to make a chart to guide the discussion.

Your Name	Your Group	What You Do	How It Helps
Marika	soccer team	run fast and kick the ball	sends ball toward other team's goal
Tony	Boy Scouts	put folding chairs away at end of meeting	cleanup is faster and easier; group gets home on time
Benjamin	this class	sweep floor and throw trash away	keeps room clean so no one trips

Hold up the book and explain that it tells the story of Frederick, who lives with a group of mice. Invite children to predict ways Frederick (a mouse himself) might help out in his group, such as by gathering food for winter or preparing a winter home.

This Book's Message or Theme

- ☼ Everyone has a responsibility to contribute.
- ☼ Everyone's contribution is important.

Let's Talk About It
Critical Thinking

Create a "hibernation" space in your classroom. Hang sheets over a clothesline strung across a corner of your classroom, or use large cardboard boxes to create a small space. Crowd your entire class into the space. Ask children to pretend they are Frederick and his friends. Say:

- ☼ **You are going to spend the whole winter here. What will you do to pass the time? What games will you play?**

- ☼ **Might you tell jokes or stories? Sing songs?**

- ☼ **What will you do to help others feel happy?**

Talk About the Story   Reading ◆ Language Arts

Talk about the contributions of Frederick and his friends. Ask:

- ☼ What did the mice do to prepare for winter? Why?
- ☼ What did Frederick do to get ready for winter?
- ☼ Why did Frederick think it was important to gather sunrays, colors, and words?
- ☼ Pretend you are a mouse who is working hard to gather food. You see that Frederick just sits. How do you feel? Why?
- ☼ Pretend it is winter. You are cold and hungry. Frederick talks about colors. Is he helping you? Why do you think that?

Mouse Mini-Book   Critical Thinking ◆ Language Arts

Duplicate and hand out the reproducible on page 31. Then:

- ☼ Help children read each sentence and draw a picture to show what happened at that point in the story.
- ☼ Have children use the blank page to draw their own ending to the story, showing how other mice were affected by Frederick's contribution to the group.
- ☼ Ask children to cut out each page along the dotted lines, put the pages in order, and number them. Then have them use crayons or markers to decorate the cover so that it resembles a mouse.
- ☼ Have children stack the pages together, with the cover on top, and punch a hole at the end of the mouse's body. Let children bind the pages together with a piece of yarn or pipe cleaner—that also becomes Frederick's tail!
- ☼ Have children cut the top off the entire book along the outer solid black line on the cover.

Recreate Lionni's Drawings Art

Browse through the story with children, taking note of techniques the artist used to create Frederick's world. Then let children use art supplies to recreate their favorite *Frederick* scenes. Cotton balls, white paint, or torn bits of white construction paper might serve as snowflakes. Torn strips of blue, red, yellow, green, and purple tissue paper can represent the colors Frederick helps his friends imagine. Watercolors can depict winter before and after Frederick speaks. Urge children to mimic the artist's techniques, tearing paper to create mouse bodies and cutting it to make ears, rocks, and nuts.

Make a Mobile of Colors, Sunrays, and Words Science ◆ Art

Let children make a mouse mobile to gather words as Frederick did. Provide each child with construction paper. Have each child draw and cut out three mice to represent Frederick. Each should be about 4 inches high. Then:

- ☼ Punch a hole at the top of each mouse and tie an 8-inch piece of string to each hole.

- ☼ Use a 12-inch strip of sturdy cardboard as the top of the mobile. Punch three holes across it. Tie the mice at varying lengths.

- ☼ Have children label one mouse "sunrays," another "colors," and the third "words." Beneath "sunrays," children draw or write on paper strips where Frederick would have found sunrays: in a sunrise, a sunset, or reflections on water. Have them do the same for "colors" (rainbows, flowers, leaves) and "words" (Frederick's thoughts, his dreams, and conversations of other mice). Have children staple the strips to each mouse.

- ☼ Attach a small paper clip or piece of string to the top of each mobile. Hang the mobiles from the ceiling.

Create Moods With Music Music

What music might Frederick have used to evoke a response in his friends? To provide warmth? Inspiration? Excitement? Relaxation? Patriotism? Select music of various tempos and styles. Help children identify how they feel as they hear each selection. Provide drawing paper and crayons, and let children draw themselves and how they feel as they listen.

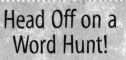

Head Off on a Word Hunt!
Language Arts

Have children read through *Frederick* in search of the many descriptive words the author used throughout the story, such as:

big	cold
little	old
gray	silly
dark	long
happy	chatty
foolish	golden

Copy onto a strip of tagboard or butcher paper each sentence that has a descriptive word, leaving a blank space where the descriptive word(s) should be. Challenge children to replace each of Lionni's descriptive words with another word that means the same thing.

Share a Poem
Language Arts

Broaden children's knowledge and appreciation of the world of mice with selections from Aileen Fisher's *The House of a Mouse* (Harper & Row, 1988), an observant collection of poems about mice, their homes, the foods they eat, and more.

Nest Testing! Science

Conduct an activity to learn how animals stay warm in cold weather. Divide the class into small groups. Give each group:

- one plastic bag
- one bucket of cold water
- feathers, grass, and leaves

Ask each group of children to place a selection of feathers, grass, and leaves inside the plastic bag. Have children take turns nestling one hand inside the bag. Ask: "Is it warm inside the bag?" (Answers may vary.) With one hand still inside, children should place the bag in cold water, being careful to keep water out. At the same time, they should dip their

other hand into the water. Ask: "How does your hand in the bag feel now? Is your hand warm or cold? How about your hand in the water?" Have children write a sentence or two to describe their findings. (The "nest" in the bag keeps out the cold, whereas the unprotected hand in the water feels the cold.) As a class, relate these findings to hibernation (for example, animals rely on fur, fat layers, and natural insulators such as leaves and feathers to keep themselves warm in cold winter months).

Books With a Similar Message or Theme

Climo, Shirley. *The Little Red Ant and the Great Big Crumb: A Mexican Fable* (Clarion Books, 1995). Considering herself too weak to move a big crumb on her own, an ant searches for someone to help her.

Pinkney, Brian. *The Adventures of Sparrowboy* (Simon & Schuster, 1997). A paperboy saves the day when he nearly collides with a sparrow and starts to fly.

Rathmann, Peggy. *Officer Buckle and Gloria* (Putnam, 1995). Officer Buckle gives lectures—but his dog Gloria steals the show. When he finally learns Gloria's secret, Officer Buckle doubts himself and wonders if his lectures are worthwhile after all.

What Happened Next?

Little by little, the mice ate their food.

Frederick gathered colors for the winter.

Frederick

Frederick spoke of sunrays and yellow wheat.

The mice gathered nuts and berries.

The Biggest House in the World
by Leo Lionni

The Biggest House in the World

(PANTHEON, 1968)

About the Book

A little snail learns the value of living simply when he hears the unfortunate story of a snail who tried to have the biggest house of all.

Before You Read

Make a Snail Chart

Show children the cover of *The Biggest House in the World* and ask them to name the animal they see. Without reading the story, invite them to tell what they know about snails, answering these questions:

☼ Have you ever seen a snail? Where did you see it?

☼ Where might you look to find a snail? Why would you look there?

☼ What do you think snails eat?

☼ How do snails travel from place to place?

☼ When might a snail need its shell?

Make a three-column chart on chart paper or the chalkboard. Label the first column "What We Think About Snails." Label the second column "What We Notice About Snails" and the third column "What We Know About Snails." As children answer the above questions, write their remarks in the first column of the chart, under the heading "What We Think About Snails." Save the chart for completion after you have shared the story.

Talk About the Story Language Arts

Talk about *The Biggest House in the World*. Ask:

☼ Why do you think the little snail wanted to have the biggest house in the world?

☼ Why did the snail's father tell him to keep his house small?

☼ How did the little snail make his house grow and be colorful?

☼ What did others say about the snail's big house?

☼ How did the little snail feel when his house was finished? Why did he feel that way?

☼ How did the little snail feel when he could not move to get food or water? Why?

☼ Did the snail do the right thing by making such a big house? Why do you say that?

Read and Research Science

Reread *The Biggest House in the World* and let the children study the illustrations. What can they learn about snails by studying the artist's work? Display the chart children started earlier. Under the heading "What We Notice About Snails," write observations that children make about snail life, based on the story and its illustrations. These observations might include:

☼ Snails live in gardens.

☼ Snails live among trees and grass.

☼ Snails eat cabbage leaves.

☼ Snails have striped shells.

☼ Snail shells are coiled.

Provide children with research materials such as fiction books about snails, encyclopedias, wildlife magazines, animal treasuries, and so on. (*The Snail's Spell* by Joanne Ryder, [Viking Penguin, 1982] is a magical book about a snail that combines fact with fantasy.) Divide the class into groups of four or six. Ask each group to find one or two facts about snails, and use these facts to complete the third column of the chart. Be sure to cover important topics such as what a snail eats, how it travels from place to place, and for what purpose it uses a shell.

Let's Talk About It
Critical Thinking

Help children identify the main message of *The Biggest House in the World*:

Don't try to be the biggest or the best. Be yourself.

On chart paper or on the chalkboard, write the message in children's words. Invite children to tell what it means and to talk about times when people might try to be the biggest or the best or to own the biggest or best possessions. Invite them to name books or movies in which characters set out to be the biggest or the best. Talk about what happened to those characters, and why they might have been better off just being themselves. For example, in the Disney version of *Aladdin*, the evil Jafar seeks to be the most powerful genie in the world . . . and ends up locked in a lamp. How might the story have ended differently if Jafar had kept different goals in mind?

Study a Snail Science

If possible, bring in several live snails for children to study. (Check your local pet store or order from Carolina Biological Supply Company, 800-334-5551). Place the snails in a terrarium with leaves, twigs, and grass, and invite children to gather around and look in. Ask them to tell what they notice about the snail, such as the color, design, or texture of its shell or the smooth, shiny surface of its body. Provide drawing paper and pencils for sketching. Invite children to study the snail and sketch its likeness on paper.

Keep On Going! Math

Reproduce page 37 and distribute to children. Have each student continue the pattern shown in each row. Then have them create their own shell patterns in the last two rows, leaving the shell at the end of each row for classmates to complete, continuing the pattern.

A Job for a Snail Social Studies

The little snail worked hard to build such a big and beautiful house. What a shame that he met an unfortunate end! Ask children to save the snail by brainstorming job possibilities for him—work the snail could offer in exchange for food. Ask children to write up mock newspaper advertisements or design WANTED posters, briefly explaining the job they have in mind.

What Really Happened? Language Arts

Reproduce page 38 and distribute. Have children read the sentences and circle only the events that took place in the story. Ask children to add, at the bottom of the page, two more details from the story. Answers: 1, 3, 4, 6, and 7.

Make a Papier-Mâché Snail Shell Art

Have children don smocks, and then make and decorate "the biggest house in the world," using papier-mâché! To do this:

☼ Cover work surfaces with newspaper. Mix flour and water to form a paste of medium thickness. Paste that is too thick will be difficult to work with. Paste that is too thin will be runny and wet.

☼ Have children tear newspaper into strips approximately 8 inches long and 1 inch wide.

☼ Blow up a balloon, and use masking tape to attach cone-shaped forms to it (paper cups with pointed ends, sugar ice cream cones, plastic foam cones, or lightweight cardboard rolled into cones and taped closed). Tape the cones to the balloon, making sure the pointed ends stick out.

☼ Dip each paper strip into the paste. Slide the paper between the index and middle finger to wipe off excess fluid. Then drape it over the model.

☼ Continue doing this until the entire model is covered. Layer well in all areas, but don't overdo it! Two or three layers work well.

☼ Sculpt the model into the shape of a snail by pressing down on the bottom to make a flat foot or pinching antennae from the paper near the head. If you prefer, you may attach pipe-cleaner antennae after the snail is dried and decorated.

☼ When the model is dry, invite children to paint the shell with poster paint or thick tempera paints. Paint a solid layer of color, such as white, first. When this layer dries, let children use thinner brushes and favorite colors to add stripes, swirls, and other designs.

Head Off on a Word Hunt! Language Arts

Challenge children to read through the story and find items they might see on a nature walk. These include:

leaves	stems
earth	pebbles
crystals	sand
sun	lichen
breeze	rocks
mushrooms	bark
flowers	trees
pinecone	buds
ferns	dew

Snail's Pace

Maybe it's so
that snails are slow:
they trudge along
and tarry.

But isn't it true
you'd slow up, too,
if you had a house
to carry?

—Aileen Fisher

After reading the poem aloud, take your class outside and invite children to move slowly, as if they were snails carrying heavy shells on their backs. Then ask them to act out other slow-moving animals, such as turtles and worms. Finally, ask children to move as faster animals, such as rabbits or horses. Back inside, ask children to draw and cut out pictures of the animals they acted out. Help them conduct research to create a display in which they order the animals from slowest to fastest.

Details, Details! Art

Ask children to bring in from home (or go on a nature hike to find) some of the natural items featured in *The Biggest House in the World*, such as pinecones, ferns, leaves, rocks, and flowers. Display these for children to study. Then help them compare real-life natural objects to Leo Lionni's artistic version. Ask: "How alike are they? How closely did the artist pay attention to details? Which details did he include? Which did he change or leave out?" Hint: Examples that show great attention to real-life detail include the veins in leaves, the holes in pebbles, and the shape and density of a pinecone.

Next, challenge children to create their own illustrations based on real-life models. Collect leaves, pebbles, or even classroom objects, such as pencils or notebooks. Guide children as they study the items and sketch them. Reassure budding artists that success in art is similar to success in any other area: It requires practice, practice, practice!

Animal Homes Social Studies ◆ Art

Help children research different animal homes. Even children who can't read can consult animal encyclopedias, wildlife magazines, or colorful books on the subject of animal homes or specific animals. Then divide the class into groups of two to four. Assign or let each group choose a different animal and use art supplies to create its home. Set the homes on a flat surface in the classroom for a museum-quality display of animal homes! Art supplies children might use to create their homes include leaves, moss, twigs, rocks, shells, feathers, clay, felt, newspaper, paint, string, and paper or cellophane grass (as used in holiday baskets). To provide a base on which to build, children might use shoe boxes or shoe box covers, squares of wood, or squares of sturdy cardboard.

Books With a Similar Message or Theme

Hoffman, Mary. *Henry's Baby* (Dorling Kindersley, 1993). Henry wants to belong to a group of cool boys at school, but he fears that his baby brother will ruin his chances. Come to find out, even cool boys like babies, and Henry's new friends are no exception.

McPhail, David. *Something Special* (Joy Street Books, 1988). Sam doubts he'll ever find his hidden talents, until one day he discovers he can paint.

Rathmann, Peggy. *Ruby the Copycat* (Scholastic, 1991). Ruby copies her classmate Angela and drives the girl to tears. With the help of her teacher, Ruby finds her own creative side and curbs her copycat ways.

Keep On Going!

Look at each row of snails below. Study the pattern in each row. Then draw what comes next.

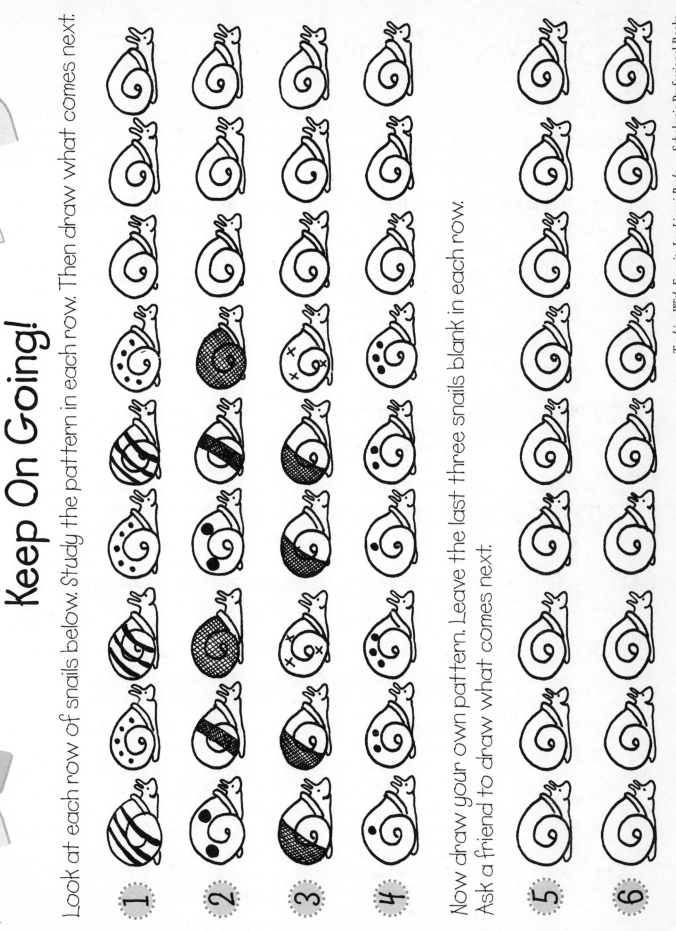

Now draw your own pattern. Leave the last three snails blank in each row. Ask a friend to draw what comes next.

Teaching With Favorite Leo Lionni Books   Scholastic Professional Books

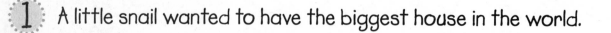

What Really Happened?

Read the sentences below. Circle the ones that tell what happened in *The Biggest House in the World.*

1 A little snail wanted to have the biggest house in the world.

2 The father snail told the little snail to try and grow a big house.

3 A little snail twisted himself to make his house grow.

4 The little snail was proud and happy when his house was big and beautiful.

5 A swarm of butterflies laughed at the little snail's house.

6 The little snail with the big house could not move to look for food.

7 The little snail who heard the story decided to keep his house small.

Now write two sentences of your own. Tell about something that happened in the story.

1 _____

2 _____

Teaching With Favorite Leo Lionni Books   Scholastic Professional Books

Fish Is Fish

(PANTHEON, 1970)

About the Book

Excited by the stories of a traveling frog, a little fish dreams about what his life would be like on land. In an attempt to make his dreams come true, he leaps onshore and quickly learns why life underwater is better for a fish.

Before You Read

Fish and Frogs Science

Prepare children for the story by reviewing basic information about fish and frogs. Share the following riddles with your class.

> I spend my life under the water.
> Fins help me swim from side to side.
> I eat small fish when I can find them.
> When big fish come, I swim or hide.
> Do you know what I am?

> My legs are long and great for leaping.
> I swim well with my webbed feet.
> I live on land and in the water.
> Bugs and worms are what I eat.
> Do you know what I am?

Read the title of the book and ask children to tell what they think the story will be about. Explain that *Fish Is Fish* is about both a fish and a frog.

This Book's Message or Theme

- ☼ Sometimes what is best for you is right before your eyes.
- ☼ Things are not always what they seem.

Invite children to recall times when they, like the fish in the story, wished they could visit a place they had never seen before. Invite them to share their experiences. Ask:

☀ **Did you ever get to the place you wanted to visit? Was it as good as you had hoped? Why do you feel that way?**

You might also focus on the present. Ask:

☀ **Do you ever wish you could visit someplace new? Where do you wish you could visit? What do you imagine it would look like?**

After You Read

Talk About the Story   Reading ♦ Language Arts

Help children focus on the similarities, differences, and friendship between the fish and the frog. Ask:

☀ How were the fish and the frog alike at the beginning of the story?

☀ In what ways did they become different from each other as they grew?

☀ How did the fish feel when he heard about the many things the frog had seen?

☀ What happened to the fish when he jumped out of the water? What did he learn from this?

☀ Was the frog a good friend to the fish? Why do you think that?

Fish or Frog? Bulletin Board   Science ♦ Critical Thinking

Using colored craft or construction paper, create an interactive pond scene on a bulletin board. Here's what to do:

1. Create a simple scene, using blue paper for the pond, green paper for lily pads, and brown paper for a shoreline.

2. Make ten or more statement pockets, using 4- by 6-inch index cards. To do this, write a factual statement on one side of each card. For example:

I live in water.	I eat fish.	I live on land.
I swim.	I have legs.	I jump.
I have fins.	I breathe through gills.	I eat bugs.
I breathe through lungs.		

3. Affix the cards to the scene with the statement side showing. Be sure to staple the cards within children's reach and staple only the sides and bottom of each card—not the top—so that it serves as a pocket.

4. Cut from sturdy tagboard the shape of a frog and that of a fish, approximately 5 inches high. Make at least 15 of each shape, and place these in a one-pound deli container, stapled to the bulletin board at a height children can reach.

5. Instruct children to use the bulletin board during free time, reading each statement (with help as needed) and placing a fish, a frog, or both into each pocket with a statement that applies to the animal.

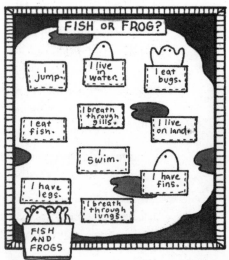

Act Out the Story Drama ◆ Language Arts

Help children recall story details and take turns at role-playing with their own stick-puppet productions of *Fish Is Fish*. Read the story aloud once more to familiarize children with the story line. Then provide them with construction paper, scissors, glue, crayons, and craft sticks or straws. Encourage them to sketch and cut out their own versions of the fish and frog featured in Leo Lionni's story, as well as some of the outlandish characters the fish imagined as the frog described birds in the sky and people and cows on land. Help children glue these characters to craft sticks or straws to make simple stick puppets, and invite them to take turns acting out the story for or with their classmates.

Postcard From a Frog Science ◆ Language Arts

Reproduce page 44 and distribute to children. Invite them to pretend they are the frog about to send a postcard to his friend, the fish. On the back of the postcard pattern, have children write or dictate a brief note from frog to fish. Ask: "What does the frog see? What would he like to tell his friend?" Then have children address the card. On the front, ask them to draw something the frog might have seen as he toured the land. When children finish, have them cut out the postcard, fold it in half, and paste together. Use a hole punch to make a hole in one corner of each completed postcard. Tie on yarn and hang the postcards from your classroom ceiling, or clip them to a clothesline strung across your classroom.

Mimic the Artist Art

As a class, review the story, taking note of illustrative techniques used in *Fish Is Fish*. The artist employed techniques that children can recreate in a simple way. For example:

☼ Have children create water scenes by placing white paper over a rough surface, such as cardboard or pressboard, and rubbing (peeled) crayons across it.

☼ Children might make leaf prints by painting leaves with tempera paint and pressing them on paper.

Head Off on a Word Hunt!
Language Arts

Send children searching for the action words (verbs) in *Fish Is Fish!* Note both past and present tense. Some verbs they might find are:

swam	climbed
grew	discovered
argued	jumped
talked	landed
groaned	pushed
floated	breathed
fly	eat
carry	

List the words as children name them. Then invite children to choose four verbs from the list and write sentences using these verbs. Depending on the skill levels of the children in your class, you may want to have them use the words to write a brief story.

☀ For simplest effect, children can color with crayon over a previously colored area, reversing the direction of the strokes to achieve a crosshatched effect.

☀ After examining the birds that the little fish imagined in the story, children may wish to sketch their own fish-based animals. Help them draw basic fish and then add features such as tails, wings, horns, whiskers, and ears to turn them into animals the fish might imagine.

☀ Provide wallpaper samples, and encourage children to design, cut out, and paste clothing onto the animals they have drawn.

Which Go Together? Science ♦ Critical Thinking

Using 3- by 5-inch index cards (or paper cut to size), have children make their own animal classification cards. Divide the class into small groups, and provide each group with 18 blank cards. Ask children to work together to draw an animal on each of nine cards. They may then use the other nine cards to draw the same animals, to serve as matches for the original nine. Children should draw animals on the cards as follows:

☀ three animals that live in water (for example, fish, crabs, whales)

☀ three animals that live on land (for example, elephants, camels, foxes)

☀ three animals that live in water and on land (for example, frogs, ducks, alligators)

Once all 18 cards have been drawn, children can shuffle the cards and take turns sorting them by location (water, land, water and land). They might also use the cards to play conventional card games such as Go Fish or Concentration. Keep the cards on hand for use during free time and at recess on bad-weather days.

The Great Divide Math

A fish is a fish, be it a live one or a cracker! Reinforce math skills—and the theme of the story—with goldfish-shaped crackers. Divide the class into pairs. Give each pair of children 20 goldfish on a paper towel. Ask them to count the fish and divide them between the two children. Ask: "How many fish do you each get?" Then combine pairs so there are four in each group.

Using only one pair's portion of goldfish, have the group divide the fish among the members. Ask: "Now how many does each of you get?" Again, add another pair to the group and ask children to divide the goldfish even further. Extend the activity by having children use the fish to solve simple addition and subtraction problems.

Books With a Similar Message or Theme

Carlson, Nancy. *Louanne Pig in Making the Team* (Carolrhoda, 1985). Louanne Pig gives cheerleading tryouts her all, but doesn't make the squad. Her good friend Arnie has the same misfortune with football. In time, the tables are turned: Louanne dons football gear while Arnie cheers on the sidelines.

Welch, Willy. *Playing Right Field* (Scholastic, 1995). A young boy stands in the outfield and dreams of the day when he'll make a great catch. All of a sudden, he does.

Young, Ed. *Mouse Match* (Silver Whistle/Harcourt Brace, 1997). A mother and father mouse seek the perfect suitor for their young daughter. After seeking the most powerful suitors in the world, they realize that a mouse is actually the best choice.

Share a Poem
Language Arts

In *Fish Is Fish*, the main character eventually decided that his underwater home was the best place for him. Help children recall this detail from the story. Then write the following poem on chart paper and read it aloud. Ask each child to draw and write or dictate why his or her home is the very nicest place (for the student) to be. Note: You may wish to elaborate on this activity by asking children to list a variety of animals and the homes they live in, such as bee (hive), bird (nest), fox (den), and so on.

The Very Nicest Place

The fish lives in the
   brook,
The bird lives in the
   tree,
But home's the very
   nicest place
For a little child
   like me.

—Anonymous

Postcard From a Frog

Front of postcard: Draw picture

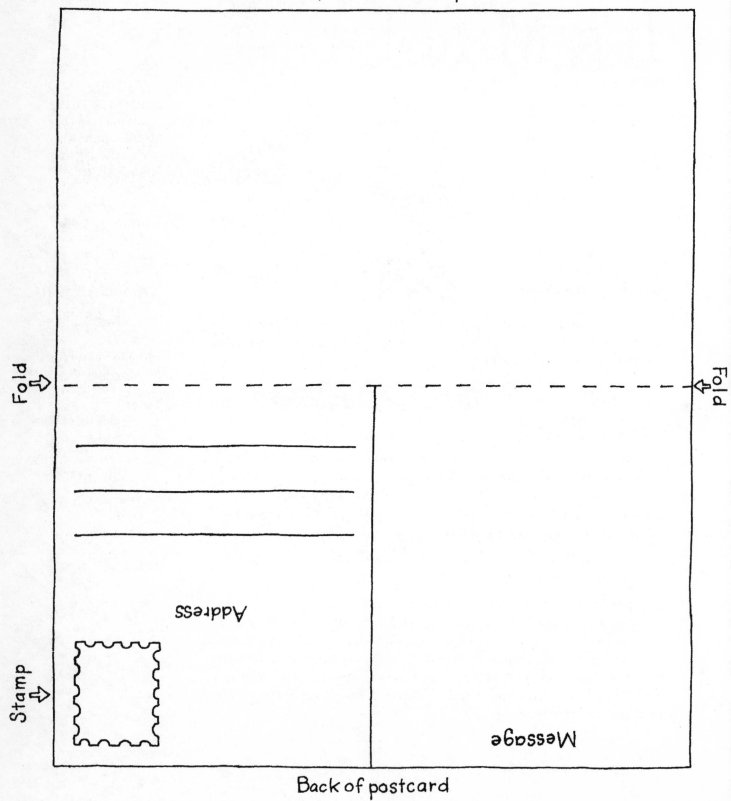

Fold ⇨

Fold ⇦

Address

Stamp ⇩

Message

Back of postcard

Teaching With Favorite Leo Lionni Books   Scholastic Professional Books

It's Mine!

(KNOPF, 1986)

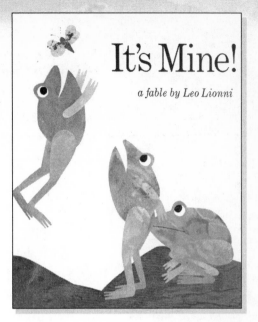

It's Mine!
a fable by Leo Lionni

About the Book

Three selfish frogs spend their days fighting over air, water, and land until a heavy storm brings them together in fear—and shows them how important it is to share and work together.

Before You Read

A Need to Share Social Studies

Ask children to tell what it means to share. By this age, they will probably realize from personal experience that sharing means giving or receiving part of something. Ask children how they feel about sharing:

☀ Is it important to share? Why do you think that?
☀ How do you feel when someone shares with you?
☀ How do you feel when someone won't share?

Talk about times when it is very important to share, such as when someone has left at home an item needed at school (for example, a lunch box or a book). Display *It's Mine!* and read the title aloud. Invite children to predict what the story will be about.

This Book's Message or Theme

☀ We need each other.
☀ It's best to share and get along.
☀ Air, land, and water belong to everyone.

Let's Talk About It
Critical Thinking

In the story *It's Mine!*, Milton, Rupert, and Lydia quarreled from dawn to dusk. How much better their lives would have been if they had learned to share— and to resolve conflicts peacefully! Take this opportunity to reinforce peaceful conflict resolution with children. Describe a conflict situation, and invite them to discuss and then draw a peaceful resolution. Conflict situations you might pose include:

☀ Someone bumps into you outside. You drop a book you are holding. It lands in a puddle.

☀ You are waiting in line at the water fountain. Someone cuts ahead of you in line.

☀ Both you and a friend want to use yellow clay. There is only one piece left.

After You Read

Talk About the Story   Reading ♦ Language Arts

Talk with children about the main elements of the story. Ask:

☀ Why did Milton, Rupert, and Lydia argue so much?

☀ Who told the frogs to stop arguing? Why did the toad want them to stop?

☀ What did the frogs do when the storm came and water flooded the land?

☀ How did the frogs feel when they huddled together? Why did they feel that way?

☀ What is the most important lesson the frogs learned in this story?

Make a Hanging Time Line
Language Arts ♦ Critical Thinking

Divide the class into groups of 4 or 6. Provide each group with six 3-inch circles (or, for a colorful twist, pieces of green paper cut in the shape of a frog) and one 24-inch strip of flat gift-wrapping ribbon. Have children work together to identify six events in the story and to draw one event on each circle. Placing the ribbon vertically on a desk, have children glue the circles onto the ribbon in the sequence the events took place in the story, making a time line of story events. Have children glue the circles approximately 2 inches apart. Hang the mobiles when the glue dries. If the ribbon will not hang straight, tape time lines flat against a wall or staple them to a bulletin board.

Make Your Own Math Problems   Math

Let children look through *It's Mine!* and use the illustrations to create their own math problems. Math problems they might write include:

1 frog + 2 frogs = 3 frogs

3 rocks - 2 rocks = 1 rock

2 butterflies + 6 butterflies = 8 butterflies

2 red flowers + 1 yellow flower = 3 flowers

Pond-Life Pantomime Drama • Critical Thinking

Reread the story aloud. Then divide the class into groups of four or six. Ask each group to act out the story in pantomime, showing without speaking what happened. You might want to demonstrate the concept first by pantomiming simple activities such as brushing teeth, dropping a box filled with heavy items, waving good-bye, and answering and talking on the telephone.

To help build the idea that pantomime is more like storytelling than like charades, ask children to note not only what you are doing but how you are feeling in the pantomime. For example, when waving good-bye, you might appear sad. This could mean that someone very special is leaving. If children have never done pantomime before, let them choose only a portion of the story to act out. Classmates can watch the pantomime and guess which part of the story the group is presenting.

Make a 3-D Frog Art ♦ Science ♦ Language Arts

Reproduce pages 49–50 for each student. Then have children:

☼ Use the Secret Code Key to decode the message on the frog's tongue, and write the answer in the blanks.

☼ Color and cut out Frog 1 and 2, the butterfly, and the frog's tongue.

☼ Roll up the frog's tongue and then glue one end onto Frog 2, as shown.

☼ Glue the butterfly to the tip of the tongue.

☼ Place Frog 1 over Frog 2, colored side up. Staple along the top of the frog's head to make a lift-the-flap book with a pop-up tongue and coded message inside.

Draw Rainbow Pond Science ♦ Art

Provide children with drawing paper and crayons. Ask them to draw Rainbow Pond and the island. Be sure to provide resources (picture books, animal magazines, and wildlife encyclopedias) that show pond life. (*One Small Square: Pond* by Donald M. Silver and Patricia J. Wynne [McGraw Hill, 1998] is an excellent resource.) Children can look at these and glean information about pond life that will enrich their drawings, such as the names of flowers, bugs, and fish found in ponds.

Head Off on a Word Hunt!
Language Arts

Go back through the story with children. Ask them to find words that show the manner in which a character spoke. These include:

yelled	**shouted**
screamed	**said**
cried	**croaked**
asked	

As a class or independently, children can choose three of the words from the above list and use each word in a sentence, complete with quotation marks.

47

Frog Song

On a lily-pad throne,
You float like a king.
Then when it gets
    dusky,
You start to sing:
Ribbity-ribbit,
croakity-croak,
Ribbity-ribbit,
croakity-croak—
I love every
    sandpaper note!

—Liza Charlesworth

Read the poem aloud. Then explain to children that animals have different ways of finding partners. Different kinds of frogs, for example, use special calls to find each other. To illustrate this for children, try this: Copy each of the frog calls below on two or three slips of paper and give one to each child. (Every two or three children should get the same call.) Tell children to walk slowly around the room, making their call. At the same time, they should try to locate another frog or frogs with the same call.

Activity adapted from Scholastic SuperScience Blue magazine, February 1996.

Pressed Leaf Pictures Art • Science

In *It's Mine!*, the island is filled with ferns and leafy weeds. Take children on a nature hike to find their own ferns, weeds, or tree leaves. Then:

- Have children place their leaves between paper towels and press them between the pages of telephone books. Put heavy books on top, and wait several weeks for the leaves to dry.

- Lay out a thick layer of newspaper and an iron. Turn the iron to a low setting, and keep it out of children's reach. One at a time, children can lay a piece of waxed paper (approximately 8 1/2 by 11 inches) on the newspaper and arrange their leaves on top of it. Children may want to use different leaf shapes to create frogs and other animals.

- Place another same-size piece of waxed paper over this, lay more newspaper on top, and iron gently for several minutes.

- Have children glue 1/2-inch strips of construction paper along the edges to serve as a frame, if desired. Tape the pictures to a window for all to enjoy!

Books With a Similar Message or Theme

Carlson, Nancy. *How to Lose All Your Friends* (Viking, 1994). Sage advice on the best ways to drive away friends: wear a big frown, never share toys, and act like a bully.

Havill, Juanita. *Jamaica's Blue Marker* (Houghton Mifflin, 1995). Jamaica is reluctant to share her markers with Russell, but she does anyway. When Russell scribbles on her picture, Jamaica learns an important lesson in forgiveness as well as generosity.

Lewin, Betsy. *Chubbo's Pool* (Clarion Books, 1996). A selfish hippo refuses to share his pool and learns an important lesson.

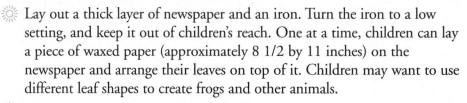

Spotted chorus frog
wrrrank, wrrank, wrrrank

Spring peeper
peep! peep! peep!

Narrow-mouthed toad
NEEEE! NEEEE!

Bullfrog
o-rum, jug-o-rum,
o-rum

Cricket frog
gick, gick

Pig frog
woink, woink, woink

Green tree frog
hey baby, baby!
hey baby, baby!

barking tree frog
arf! arf! arf!

Squirrel tree frog
quank, quank

Make a 3-D Frog

Can you crack the frog's secret code? Try it! Then make your own 3-D frog!

1 Look at each picture in the secret code below.

2 Check the Secret Code Key to find out what letter each picture stands for.

3 Write the letter on the blank line above the picture. The first one has been done for you.

Secret Code Key

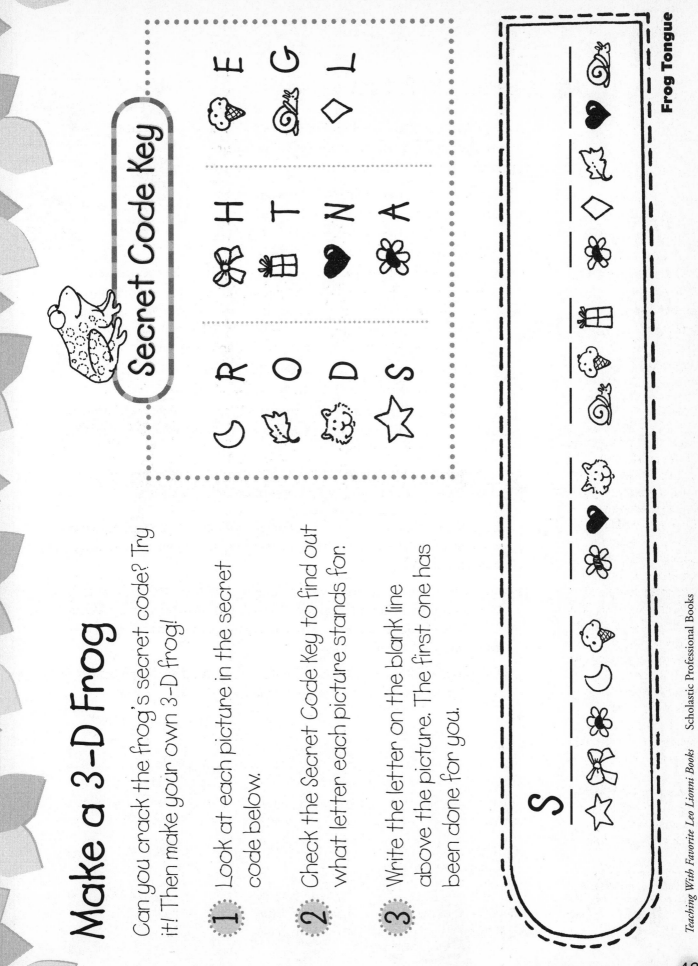

R   O   D   S   E   G   L   H   T   N   A

Frog Tongue

S

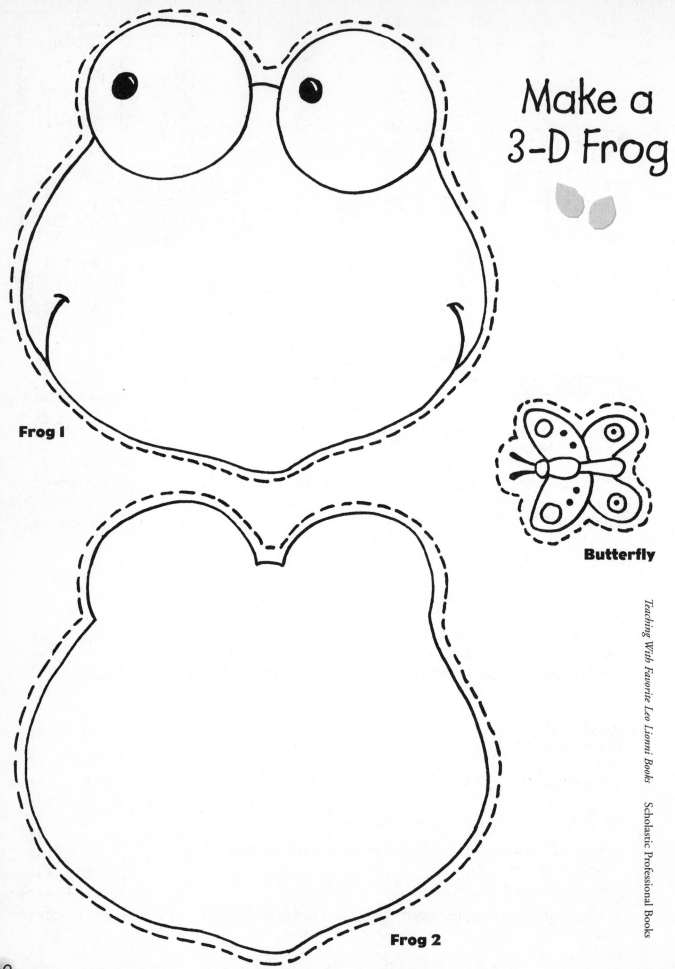

Make a 3-D Frog

Frog 1

Frog 2

Butterfly

Teaching With Favorite Leo Lionni Books   Scholastic Professional Books

Nicolas, Where Have You Been?

(KNOPF, 1987)

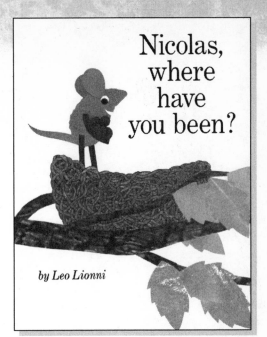

Nicolas, where have you been?

by Leo Lionni

About the Book

An unexpected stay in a bird's nest leads a young mouse to realize that not all birds are the enemies he once thought.

Before You Read

Make Predictions Critical Thinking

Hold up the cover of the book and ask children to tell what they see. They are likely to notice that a mouse is standing inside a bird's nest. Invite them to predict what the story will be about. For example, they might think the mouse is taking berries from the nest. They might predict that he believes he is a bird or that he is using an abandoned bird's nest for a house.

After You Read

Talk About the Story Reading ♦ Language Arts

After reading the story, take time to bring out the main ideas. Ask:

- How did Nicolas feel about birds at the beginning of the story? Why did he feel that way?
- Why did Nicolas set out on his own?
- What frightening thing happened to him when he was in the grass?

This Book's Message or Theme

- Sometimes others aren't what they seem.

Note: This book is out of print. Check your library for a circulating copy.

Let's Talk About It
Critical Thinking

Remind children that in the story, the mice said, "Down with birds! War on the birds!" and actually pictured themselves fighting with the birds. What might have happened if Nicolas had not intervened? Fortunately, Nicolas eased their anger with his words and prevented a battle. Discuss conflict and resolution by having the class respond to these two statements: Brooding on anger can make people act in a more angry manner than they might otherwise; and kind words, attitudes, and explanations can appease others' anger and prevent conflict. Invite children to tell about or draw situations in which they have been able to calm themselves or others and prevent a potentially harmful situation. Encourage children to be peacemakers as Nicolas ended up being; urge them to seek the good in others and make it known.

☀ How did Nicolas feel about the birds who let him stay in their nest? Why do you say that?

☀ How did the other mice feel when they learned that Nicolas had been taken away by a bird? What did they want to do?

☀ How did Nicolas get rid of his friends' anger?

☀ What did Uncle Raymond mean when he said, "One bad bird doesn't make a flock"?

Help children understand the main idea of the story, which is that no one should be judged as part of a group, because they might not deserve the judgment. Invite children to come up with examples of times people or animals might be wrongly judged. For example, someone who has been bitten by a dog might believe that all dogs are mean-tempered and will bite. Someone who has been teased by older children might believe that all older children are not to be trusted. In the same way, someone who has been treated kindly by a stranger may believe that all strangers are kind and helpful, which is not true.

What Do They Eat? Science

Talk with children about the foods that Nicolas told the mother bird he liked to eat: nuts, corn, and berries. Explain that Nicolas is a field mouse, and field mice are herbivores: They eat only plants and foods grown on plants. They do not eat other animals or any type of meat.

Reproduce and distribute page 56. Explain that children are going to make a food wheel that shows the kinds of foods field mice eat, such as seeds, berries, hay, grass, and corn. Help children cut out and assemble the food wheel as follows:

1. Cut out each wheel along the dotted lines. Cut out the windows on Wheel A. (An easy way to cut out the inner window is to fold the paper at a right angle to the dotted lines. Then snip along the lines to the crease of the fold inward.)

2. Place Wheel A on top of Wheel B. Insert a brass fastener through the center dot, and fasten.

3. Have children draw one food item in each section of Wheel B.

Allow time for children to use their food wheels. Then talk about foods that other kinds of mice, such as the common house mouse, might eat. These foods might include cheese, crackers, dog bones, cereal, and so on.

Recreate Scenes From the Story Art

Revisit the story, and encourage children to look carefully at the illustrations. Invite children to tell what medium the author used to create the art. Did he use paint? Colored pencil? Cut paper? Markers? Challenge children to work in the style of Leo Lionni's artwork by using the techniques they think give Lionni's illustrations their special look. Provide scissors, colored craft paper, wallpaper, large sheets of white construction paper, and glue. Ask children to work independently or in small groups to recreate one scene in the story, using cut paper to make animal legs, leaves, and terrain. When children have finished, invite them to show their scenes to the class, challenging classmates to guess which part of the story each scene depicts.

Ripe Versus Unripe Science

In the story, the mice complained that birds were eating all the ripe, red berries and leaving them with pale ones that weren't ripe. Conduct a taste test to help children compare fruits at different stages and gain a clearer understanding of why the mice were so upset. Bring in samples of ripe and unripe fruit, such as bananas, tomatoes, melon, apples, and pineapple. Cut fruit into pieces and let children compare ripe and unripe samples of each kind. Make a chart to compare the fruits by color, hardness, flavor, and smell. Ask children which fruit they prefer (ripe or unripe) and why they think the mice were upset at having only unripe berries. NOTE: Before doing this activity, check with parents about any possible food allergies children might have.

Name of Fruit	Color	Hard or Soft	Flavor	Smell
Ripe banana	yellow	soft	sweet	strong
Unripe banana	green & yellow	hard	bitter	faint
Ripe canteloupe	orange	soft	sweet	strong & sweet
Unripe canteloupe	green	hard	not much flavor	faint
Ripe apple	red	hard	sweet	strong apple
Unripe apple	red & green	hard	chalky; not much flavor	faint apple smell

Head Off on a Word Hunt! Language Arts

Challenge children to reread the story and find sentences or phrases that convey emotion. Have children read aloud each sentence and identify the emotion behind it. Some of the phrases children might find include:

"That's not fair!" (frustration)

"Down with the birds!" (anger)

"Nicolas couldn't believe his eyes." (surprise, amazement)

"Nicolas ate berries to his heart's content." (satisfaction, contentment)

"... but Nicolas was too sad to eat." (sadness)

"Fearfully he climbed down the tree ..." (fear)

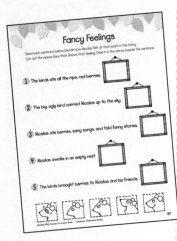

Fancy Feelings Language Arts • Social Studies

Reproduce page 57 and distribute. Help children read the directions and cut out the mouse faces at the bottom of the page. Provide glue and ask them to glue each mouse expression beside the sentence that describes it.

Write a Letter Language Arts

Remind children that while he was with the birds, Nicolas was away from his friends for quite a while. They must have been worried! As a class, in groups, or independently, children can pretend to be Nicolas and write a letter home to his friends, letting them know how he is doing.

Dear Friends,

Do not worry about me. I am safe! I am singing songs with my new bird friends. I have plenty to eat and a warm place to sleep. I'll see you soon!

Your friend,
Nicolas

Berry Math! Math

Conduct a math activity with ripe, red berries: cranberries! Divide the class into pairs. Give each pair of children 10 to 20 uncooked cranberries in a paper cup. Let children use the berries as they wish to make math problems for each other to solve. (Use the natural dye in cranberries to make a permanent record of these problems. Cut the berries in half and let children stamp them on paper to make prints!) For example, one partner might:

☼ Place two berries on a desk and then add six more. His or her partner can then write the sum on a piece of paper as 2 + 6 = 8.

☼ Place all the berries on a desk and ask his or her partner to separate the berries into two or three equal groups.

☼ Divide the berries into groups of two and write a multiplication sentence: 2 berries in each of 10 groups equals 20 berries.

Make Story Viewers Art ◆ Language Arts

Provide children with long strips of adding machine paper. Have them draw scenes from the story, in chronological order. Children may wish to draw their own story in lieu of a retelling. Encourage them to create a story similar in theme to *Nicholas, Where Have You Been?*, telling about a person or animal who learns that a supposed enemy is really a friend. When the stories are finished, show children how to make a homemade projector to share their stories:

☀ Provide each child with a clean, empty milk carton (pint or half-pint size). Help children cut open the bottom of the carton, then cut a 2 1/2-inch slit in each side as shown.

☀ To view their stories, have students thread the strip through the slits in the carton and pull the strip through the projector. Invite children to share their stories with classmates.

Share a Poem
Language Arts

Both feathered and furry animals frolic across the pages of Aileen Fisher's poetry collection *Feathered Ones and Furry* (Thomas Y. Crowell, 1971). These easy-to-read poems, filled with observant details about animals such as robins and wrens and mice and chipmunks, will fascinate children and encourage them to take a closer look at the wildlife living outside their window.

Books With a Similar Message or Theme

Bang, Molly. *The Paper Crane* (Greenwillow, 1985). Despite hard times, a restaurant owner and his son feed a poor passerby one evening. In return for their kindness, the man gives the boy a magical gift that saves the restaurant from closing.

Trivizas, Eugene. *The Three Little Wolves and the Big Bad Pig* (Margaret K. McElderry Books, 1993). An angry pig wreaks havoc on the homes of three little wolves until the pig realizes the error of his ways.

Henkes, Kevin. *Sheila Rae, the Brave* (Greenwillow, 1987). Brave Sheila Rae doesn't feel very brave when she gets lost coming home from school. Luckily, her timid young sister Louise knows the way and turns out to be fearless herself.

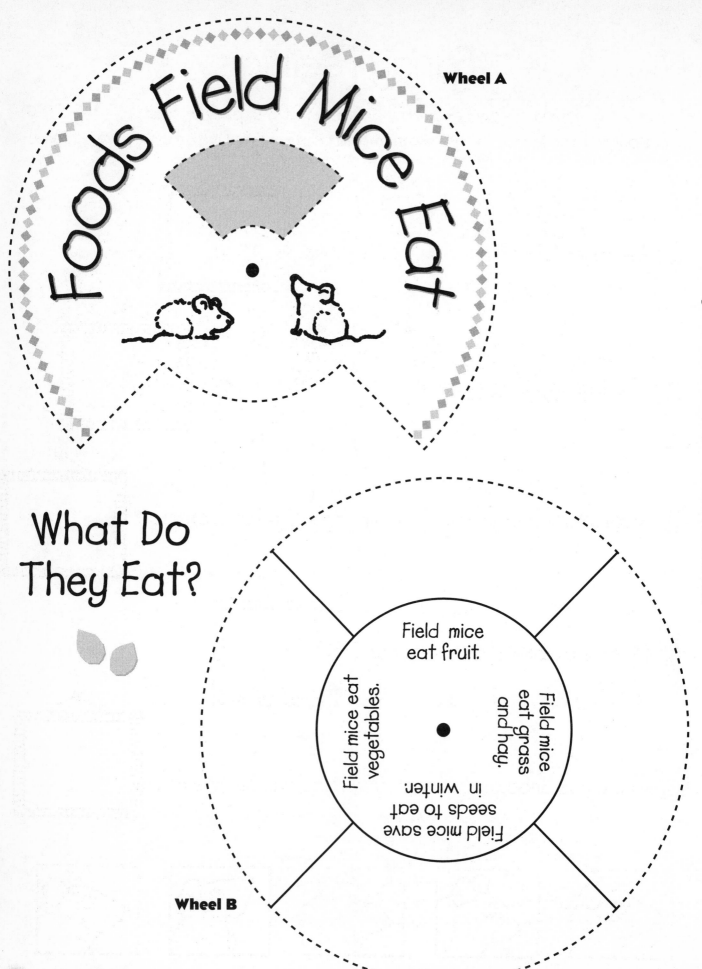

Wheel A

Foods Field Mice Eat

What Do They Eat?

Field mice eat fruit.

Field mice eat grass and hay.

Field mice save seeds to eat in winter.

Field mice eat vegetables.

Wheel B

Fancy Feelings

Read each sentence below. Decide how Nicolas felt at that point in the story.
Cut out the mouse face that shows that feeling. Glue it in the mirror beside the sentence.

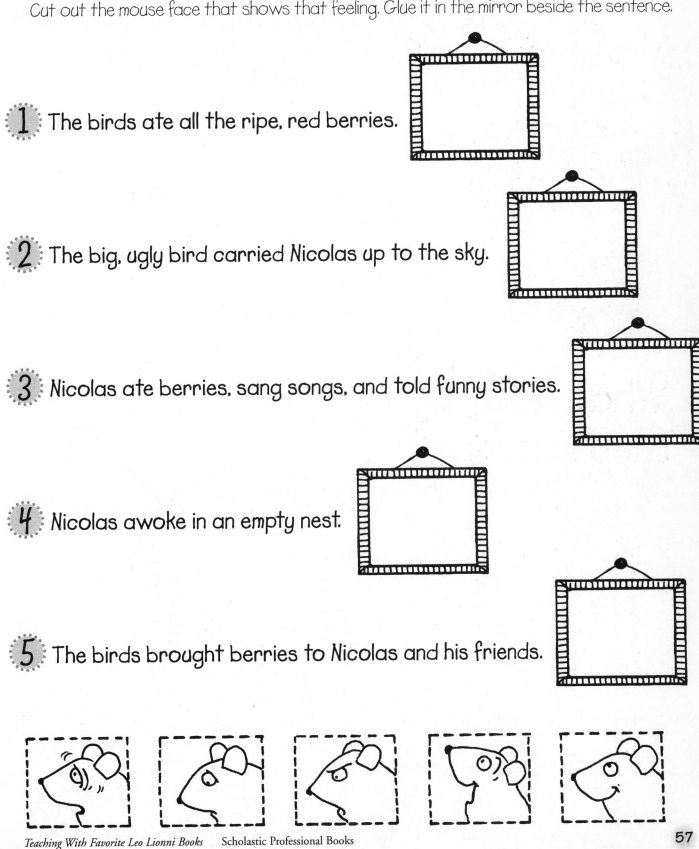

1 The birds ate all the ripe, red berries.

2 The big, ugly bird carried Nicolas up to the sky.

3 Nicolas ate berries, sang songs, and told funny stories.

4 Nicolas awoke in an empty nest.

5 The birds brought berries to Nicolas and his friends.

Ideas for Use With Other Books by Leo Lionni

Use the following activities to bring more of Leo Lionni's books to life in your classroom.

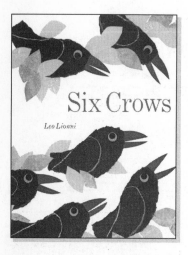

Six Crows

(KNOPF, 1988)

Six crows and a farmer frighten each other away from a wheat field until a wise owl teaches them to talk it out and resolve their differences.

▲▲▲▲▲▲▲▲▲▲▲▲▲▲▲▲▲▲▲▲▲▲▲▲▲▲

Interview the Characters Divide the class into groups of five or six. Let some children play the role of reporters and interview classmates posing as the farmer, the crows, and the owl in *Six Crows*. Have children record the interviews on cassette tape and play them for the class. Encourage children to react to events that actually happened in the story, sharing their emotions as the plot unfolded.

Chalk It Up! Revisit *Six Crows* and invite children to pay attention to details in the artwork and speculate on the artist's techniques. For example, they might say:

"I think Leo Lionni...

...used chalk to draw wings on the birds."

...glued black paper on orange circles to make the birds' eyes."

...glued feathers on the bird to make a collage."

Let children experiment with the techniques they think the artist used. Suggestions include:

- **Draw with chalk on construction paper** Have children cut out animal shapes and draw the features with dry chalk or chalk that has been dipped in water.
- **Make an animal collage** Let students cut or tear the shape of an animal from construction paper. Have them cut leaves (or other shapes) from tissue paper and glue them to the animal to cover it, much like the birds covered their kites.
- **Use cut paper to make scarecrows** Provide colored paper and let children design, cut out, and glue together their own miniature scarecrows. Mount the scarecrows on craft sticks and display them on a bulletin board of yellow paper wheat.

People Use Wheat Discuss the idea that the farmer worked hard to defend his field from the crows because wheat is a valuable crop. With children's help, list some of the ways people use wheat. As a class, make a graph of foods containing wheat that children have eaten so far today. Draw tally marks beside each food item to show how many children have eaten it.

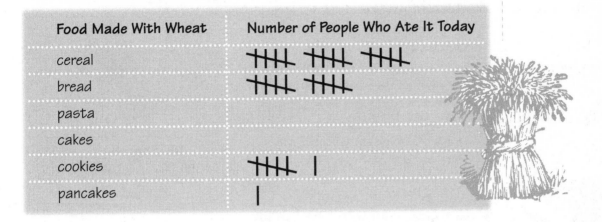

Food Made With Wheat	Number of People Who Ate It Today
cereal	~~IIII~~ ~~IIII~~ ~~IIII~~
bread	~~IIII~~ ~~IIII~~
pasta	
cakes	
cookies	~~IIII~~ I
pancakes	I

Alexander and the Wind-Up Mouse

(PANTHEON, 1969)

A real mouse wishes he could be a toy so that people will love him instead of chasing him away. When given a magic wish, the real mouse makes a surprising choice.

▲▲▲▲▲▲▲▲▲▲▲▲▲▲▲▲▲▲▲▲▲▲▲▲▲

Make It Move! People and animals use their own energy to move from place to place. Objects such as toys rely on other energy sources to make them move. Bring in examples of movable toys that operate on energy provided by winding mechanisms, batteries, electricity, and so on. With your supervision, let children use the toys and explore different ways to generate motion.

Graph Wind-Up Races Let children wind up and watch them go! Place tape on the floor to mark a racetrack in 6-inch increments. Hold races to find out which wind-up toys travel farthest. Log the results on a graph.

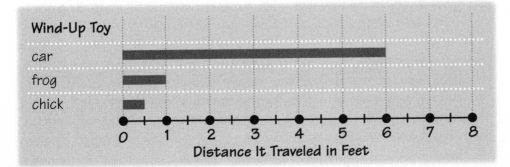

Write a Wind-Up Story Divide the class into small groups. Display a selection of wind-up toys, and ask each group to choose one. Ask them to hold and operate the toy and then write a fiction story about it, telling of an adventure or other experience it might have had. Be sure children illustrate their stories as well!

Marbleized Art Let children recreate the swirling patterns of color used by Lionni in some of this book's illustrations. Cover a work surface with newspaper. Fill a disposable foil baking pan halfway with very hot water and let children sprinkle crayon shavings over the surface. The heat of the water will melt the crayon. Swirl with a toothpick, then lay a piece of paper on top of the water, gently tapping the paper to cover the entire surface. Lift the paper by the edges and place on paper towels to dry.

A Flea Story

(PANTHEON, 1977)

Two friends who are fleas part ways when they discover that one wants to travel and the other does not.

▲▲▲▲▲▲▲▲▲▲▲▲▲▲▲▲▲▲▲▲▲▲▲▲▲▲

Map the Fleas' Journey Ask children to imagine where the fleas might have traveled as they rode on the dog. Divide the class into groups or let children work independently to write a travel log of places the fleas visited in their own community, within their state, or around the United States. Younger children may wish to draw a picture of one or two places the fleas saw as they traveled, such as the school, the community library, or the playground. Older children may write about the journey, naming the places they saw and landmarks they noticed at each location.

Make Travel Brochures Invite children to design a creative travel brochure to lure fleas to faraway places. Children don't have to specify the location but should focus on activities, sights, and amenities that fleas might find appealing, such as thick carpeting, warm climate, and an abundance of dogs and cats on-site.

Explore Creative Imagery Provide drawing paper and let children draw a flea riding on an animal of their choice: a bird, a duck, an elephant, a monkey, and so on. Invite them to focus on animals of various types and in a variety of locations and to imagine what it would be like to travel on the animal. You might say: "Pretend you are a flea. What would it feel like to ride on a bird?"

Compare Likes and Dislikes One flea liked to travel. The other liked to stay home. How else were the fleas in *A Flea Story* alike and different? Make a Venn diagram to show their similarities and differences.

Inch by Inch

(ASTOR-HONOR, 1960)

An inchworm measures for all kinds of animals until his life is threatened and he measures his way out of sight.

▲▲▲▲▲▲▲▲▲▲▲▲▲▲▲▲▲▲▲▲▲▲▲▲▲▲

Hunt and Measure On white paper, list ten different measurements, such as 1 inch, 12 inches, 2 feet, and so on. Reproduce the page and give one to each student. Have children work in small groups, using rulers to measure objects in the classroom and to find objects that equal the measurements you have listed. Have them write the name of each object next to its measurement. Give small rulers as prizes to the first group of children who find items for all ten measurements.

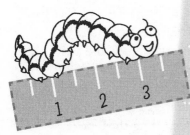

Hunt and Measure

Measurement	Object
1 inch	
3 inches	
7 inches	pencil
11 inches	notebook paper
12 inches	
18 inches	
24 inches	desk
4 feet	
6 feet	
8 feet	door

Measure With Inchworms Cut thick, light-green yarn into 4-inch strands. Glue tiny movable eyes to one end of the strand to make an inchworm. Give children one inchworm apiece and ask them to use it to measure common items in the classroom, such as desks, books, pencils, and lunch boxes.

Note the Outstanding! In *Inch by Inch*, the birds are all tall or have long features. The flamingo's neck, the toucan's beak, the heron's legs, and the pheasant's tail are all long. Invite children to guess why Leo Lionni used these birds in his story. (to emphasize length and to give the inchworm something to measure) Ask children to think of other animals that have outstanding or notable features, such as elephants, giraffes, camels, cheetahs, monkeys, alligators, and snakes. Make a chart, recording the animal's name in the left column and its outstanding feature(s) in the right.

the alphabet tree

Leo Lionni

The Alphabet Tree

(PANTHEON, 1968)

With the help of a word-bug and a caterpillar, a group of letters learns to make words and then sentences on the leaves of an alphabet tree.

▲▲▲▲▲▲▲▲▲▲▲▲▲▲▲▲▲▲▲▲▲▲▲▲▲▲▲

Make an Interactive Bulletin Board Recreate the artwork in the story by cutting out leaves and writing a letter of the alphabet on each one. Create extra leaves with vowels and the consonants most frequently found in words—*b, f, l, m, r, s,* and *t.* Laminate each leaf and affix a small piece of Velcro to the back. Then make a row of Velcro squares on the bulletin board, being careful to spread them apart so the leaves can easily fit beside each other when attached. Place the leaves in an envelope or craft paper pocket on the bulletin board. Encourage children to use the bulletin board during free time, placing the leaves side by side to make words. Use this technique to introduce new words and reinforce spelling words.

Scramble Scrabble Use letter squares from the game Scrabble.™ Turn the squares upside down and mix them up. Let children work in groups of three or four to turn over letters and combine them to make words.

Build With Sentence Blocks Cut paper or index cards to the size of classroom building blocks. Tape one to the side of each block and write on it a word children know, such as *wind, big,* or *door.* Do this to at least 20 blocks, writing one word on each block. Be sure to write nouns, verbs, and adjectives, which will allow children to form sentences. Let children work independently or in small groups to build sentences using the blocks.

Tico and the Golden Wings

(PANTHEON, 1964)

Unable to fly since birth, Tico receives a magical gift of golden wings. Rejected by his friends for such splendor, Tico gives away his features one by one, touching lives with his kindness.

▲▲▲▲▲▲▲▲▲▲▲▲▲▲▲▲▲▲▲▲▲

Award Golden Wings Tico gave away his golden feathers to help others. Like Tico, children can perform kind acts every day. Encourage and reward kindness in your classroom by awarding golden feathers for caring, considerate acts that you witness. To make gold feathers, spray-paint craft feathers or feathers cut from tagboard, or cut feathers from gold-colored craft paper.

I Was a Good Friend Give children each a golden feather. Ask each child to write or dictate a sentence that tells what he or she did recently to be a good friend to someone. Post the feathers for others to see.

Feather Countdown Waiting for a special day at school? Make a bird with golden feathers to represent each day in the waiting period. Let children pick a golden feather each day to count down until the appointed day arrives.

Words Paint Pictures Review the story with children, and invite them to listen for descriptive words and phrases as you read. Write each phrase on a separate tagboard feather. Let students each choose a feather and draw a picture of what comes to mind when they read (or hear) those words. Sample phrases include:

"The flower patches below looked like stamps scattered over the countryside."

"...the river [looked] like a silver necklace lying in the meadows."

"...on my back there were wings, golden wings, shimmering in the moonlight."

"My wings were as black as India ink."

In addition to the 13 stories featured in this book, Leo Lionni has published more than two dozen others. Expand children's appreciation of this gifted author-illustrator by sharing the following picture books:

A Busy Year (Knopf, 1992)

Mouse friends adopt a tree and then watch it grow and change with the seasons.

A Color of His Own (Pantheon, 1975)

A chameleon wishes to find and keep a color of his own. His search for this ends when he meets another chameleon and they change colors together.

Cornelius (Pantheon, 1983)

Able to walk upright, Cornelius can see far above the heads of his crocodile friends. His jealous friends reject him until one day they try seeing life from his point of view.

An Extraordinary Egg (Knopf, 1994)

Three frogs find an egg and think it belongs to a chicken. The egg hatches, and the frogs believe they are playing and talking with a chicken, which is in fact an alligator.

Geraldine, the Music Mouse (Pantheon, 1979)

Young Geraldine carves a mouse out of cheese and discovers music in her sculpture.

The Greentail Mouse (Pantheon, 1973)

Mice gather to celebrate Mardi Gras, but the masks they wear for the party cause fear and unhappiness in their small community.

In the Rabbitgarden (Pantheon, 1975)

Two rabbits play in a beautiful garden and enlist the help of a friendly serpent to protect them from a dangerous fox.

Let's Make Rabbits (Pantheon, 1982)

Two rabbits, made with pencil and scissors, become real when they eat a real carrot.

Matthew's Dream (Knopf, 1991)

Unsure what he will be when he grows up, a mouse named Matthew visits a museum and then realizes he wants to be a painter.

Mouse Days (Pantheon, 1981)

A group of mice enjoys the weather and activities unique to each season of the year.

Mr. McMouse (Knopf, 1992)

A city mouse tries to find his true identity among a group of field mice after he is transformed into a tiny man.

Theodore and the Talking Mushroom (Pantheon, 1971)

A mouse interprets the speech of a talking mushroom to serve his own needs. When the other animals in the wood discover his secret, the mouse is banished from the forest.

Tillie and the Wall (Knopf, 1989)

Tillie is determined to find out what lies on the other side of a wall she has seen all her life.